D0818570

DIVING & SNORKELING

Hawaii

Casey Mahaney

lonely planet

MELBOURNE | LONDON | OAKLAND

Hawaii

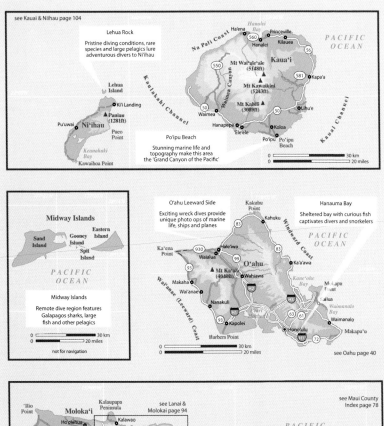

see Kauai & Niihau page 104

Lehua Rock

Pristine diving conditions, rare species and large pelagics lure adventurous divers to Ni'ihau

Hanalei Bay
Na Pali Coast
Ha'ena
Princeville
Hanalei
Kilauea
560
56
PACIFIC OCEAN
Kaua'i
550
Mt Wai'ale'ale (5148ft)
Waimea Canyon
Mt Kawaikini (5243ft)
581
Kapa'a
Kaulakahi Channel
Lehua Island
Ki'i Landing
Paniau (1281ft)
Mt Kahili (3089ft)
50
Kauai Channel
Pu'uwai
Ni'ihau
Waimea
50
Lihu'e
Pueo Point
Hanapepe
'Ele'ele
Koloa
Keanahaki Bay
Po'ipu
Po'ipu Beach
Kawaihoa Point

Po'ipu Beach

Stunning marine life and topography make this area the 'Grand Canyon of the Pacific'

0 — 30 km
0 — 20 miles

Midway Islands

Sand Island
Gooney Island
Eastern Island
Spit Island

PACIFIC OCEAN

Midway Islands

Remote dive region features Galapagos sharks, large fish and other pelagics

0 — 30 km
0 — 20 miles

not for navigation

O'ahu Leeward Side

Exciting wreck dives provide unique photo ops of marine life, ships and planes

Kahuku Point
Kahuku
83
Windward Coast
PACIFIC OCEAN

Hanauma Bay

Sheltered bay with curious fish captivates divers and snorkelers

Ka'ena Point
930
Hale'iwa
Waialua
99
83
Ka'a'awa
93
Mt Ka'ala (4040ft)
O'ahu
Wahiawa
Kane'ohe Bay
Mokapu Point
Makaha
Wai'anae
H2
Kailua
Waimanalo Bay
Nanakuli
Wai'anae (Leeward) Coast
63
61
Waimanalo
93
Kapolei
H1
Pearl Harbor
Honolulu
72
Makapu'u
Barbers Point

0 — 30 km
0 — 20 miles

see Oahu page 40

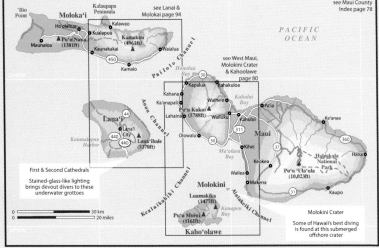

'Ilio Point
Kalaupapa Peninsula
Kalawao
see Lanai & Molokai page 94
see Maui County Index page 78

Moloka'i
Ho'olehua
Kualapuu
Kamakou (4961ft)
Kalaupapa
PACIFIC OCEAN
Maunaloa
Pu'u Nana (1381ft)
Kaunakakai
Waialua
450
Kamalo
Pailolo Channel
Honolua Bay
see West Maui, Molokini Crater & Kahoolawe page 80

30
Kapalua
Kahakuloa
Kahana
Waihe'e
Kahului Bay
Pa'ia
Ke'anae
Auau Channel
Ka'anapali
Pu'u Kukui (5788ft)
Wailuku
Kahului
360
Lana'i
44
Lahaina
311
Maui
Lana'i City
440
Olowalu
30
Kihei
37
Haleakala National Park
Kaumalapau Harbor
Lana'ihale (3370ft)
Ma'alaea Bay
Keokea
Pu'u 'Ula'ula (10,023ft)
Hana

First & Second Cathedrals

Stained-glass-like lighting brings devout divers to these underwater grottoes

Wailea
Makena
Kaupo
Kealaikahiki Channel
Molokini
Luamakika (1477ft)
Kanapou Bay
Alalakeiki Channel
31

0 — 30 km
0 — 20 miles

Pu'u Moiwi (1161ft)
Kaho'olawe

Molokini Crater

Some of Hawaii's best diving is found at this submerged offshore crater

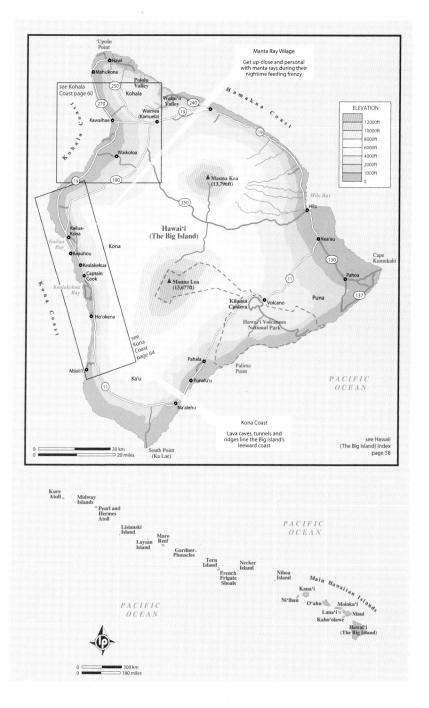

'Upolu
Point

Hawi
Mahukona

Pololu
Valley
Kohala

250

see Kohala
Coast page 60

270

Waipi'o
Valley

240

Hamakua Coast

Manta Ray Village

Get up-close and personal
with manta rays during their
nightime feeding frenzy

Waimea
(Kamuela)

Kawaihae

19

19

Kohala Coast

Waikoloa

19

190

ELEVATION

12000ft
10000ft
8000ft
6000ft
4000ft
2000ft
1000ft
0

Mauna Kea
(13,796ft)

250

Hilo Bay

Kailua-
Kona

Kailua
Bay

Keauhou

Kealakekua

Captain
Cook

Kealakekua
Bay

Hawai'i
(The Big Island)

Kona

Hilo

Kea'au

130

Cape
Kumukahi

Pahoa

137

Ho'okena

Kona Coast

see
Kona
Coast
page 64

Mauna Loa
(13,677ft)

Kilauea
Caldera

Volcano

Puna

Hawai'i Volcanoes
National Park

Miloli'i

Ka'u

11

Pahala

Punalu'u

Palima
Point

PACIFIC
OCEAN

Na'alehu

Kona Coast

Lava caves, tunnels and
ridges line the Big Island's
leeward coast

see Hawaii
(The Big Island) Index
page 58

0   30 km
0   20 miles

South Point
(Ka Lae)

Kure
Atoll

Midway
Islands

Pearl and
Hermes
Atoll

Lisianski
Island

Maro
Reef

PACIFIC
OCEAN

Laysan
Island

Gardner
Pinnacles

Tern
Island

Necker
Island

French
Frigate
Shoals

Nihoa
Island

Main Hawaiian Islands

Kaua'i

Ni'ihau

O'ahu

Moloka'i

Lana'i

Maui

Kaho'olawe

PACIFIC
OCEAN

Hawai'i
(The Big Island)

0   300 km
0   180 miles

Diving & Snorkeling Hawaii
2nd edition – September 2006

Published by
Lonely Planet Publications Pty Ltd
ABN 36 005 607 983
90 Maribyrnong St, Footscray,
Victoria, 3011, Australia
www.lonelyplanet.com

Lonely Planet Offices
Australia Locked Bag 1, Footscray, Victoria, 3011
Phone 03 8379 8000 Fax 03 8379 8111
Email talk2us@lonelyplanet.com.au

USA 150 Linden St, Oakland, CA 94607
Phone 510 893 8555 Toll free 800 275 8555 Fax 510 893 8572
Email info@lonelyplanet.com

UK 72-82 Rosebery Ave London EC1R 4RW
Phone 020 7841 9000 Fax 020 7841 9001
Email go@lonelyplanet.co.uk

Author Casey Mahaney
Publisher Roz Hopkins
Publishing Manager Chris Rennie
Commissioning Editor Ben Handicott
Design Manager Brendan Dempsey
Mapping Development Paul Piaia
Project Management Annelies Mertens
Production Pepper Publishing (Aust) Pty Ltd
Print Production Manager Graham Imeson

Printed by C&C Offset Printing Co Ltd, China
Photographs Casey Mahaney (unless otherwise noted)

ISBN 1740591291

© Lonely Planet 2006
© Photographers as indicated 2006

All rights reserved. No part of this publication may be reproduced,
stored in a retrieval system or transmitted in any form by any means,
electronic, mechanical, photocopying, recording or otherwise except
brief extracts for the purpose of review, without the written permis-
sion of the publisher. Lonely Planet and the Lonely Planet logo are
trademarks of Lonely Planet and are registered in the US patent and
Trademark Office and in other countries.

With Many Thanks to
Jennifer Bilos, Jo Vraca, Alison Lyall, Carol Chandler, Amy Carroll,
Angus Fleetwood, Tom Calderwood, Sayher Heffernan

Although the authors and
Lonely Planet have taken all
reasonable care in preparing
this book, we make no war-
ranty about the accuracy or
completeness of its content
and, to the maximum extent
permitted, disclaim all liabil-
ity from its use.

Contents

Author

CASEY MAHANEY

Casey Mahaney has been a dive industry professional since 1983. He is an internationally published author, has co-written five marine life identification guides and has also co-authored Lonely Planet/Pisces series guides to Fiji and the Maldives. Casey took up underwater photography while captaining liveaboard vessels world-wide as a licensed Coast Guard Captain. His dive travel company, Blue Kirio Travel, specializes in personalized dive tours to the world's top dive destinations. The tours cater to underwater photographers and marine-life enthusiasts, and generally utilize top rate live-aboard dive boats.

FROM THE AUTHOR

A variety of people and organizations assisted in compiling and updating this guidebook. I would like to thank every-one in the Hawaiian dive industry for their contributions of local knowledge and expertise, use of dive vessels and accommodations over the years. I would also like to give a special thanks to the following individuals for their assistance with this most recent update.

From the Big Island; Paul Warren of Hualalai Watersports, Teri Leicher, Jacks Diving Locker, Rich Kersten, Sea Paradise and Mendy Dant, Fairwind Cruises. From Maui; Eric Stein, Extended Horizons, Pauline Severens, Mike Severens Diving, Diana Madaras, Maui Dive Shop, Hannah Bernard, President Hawaii Wildlife Fund and Charley Neal, Scuba Shack Maui. From Oahu; Randy and Suzette, Captain Bruce Scuba, Bob, Oahu Dive Center, Captain Nick, Waikiki Dive Center, Devon Merrifield, Reef Trekkers Hawaii, Aqua Zone Scuba and Andre. From Kauai; Linda Marsh, Seasport Divers, Bubbles Below and Marvin Otsuji.

PHOTOGRAPHIC EQUIPMENT

Though digital photography is becoming the norm, you will find that all photographs in this book, unless noted, were taken by Casey and Astrid Mahaney using a variety of film cameras and formats.

For macro and close-up photography the Nikon 8008s and N90s fitted with either a 105mm or 60mm lens in an Ikelite housing were used. Wide-angle photographs were taken using either a Nikon 20mm or 14mm lens in a Nexus housing, or with Nikonos III and V cameras with a 15mm lens.

Topside shots were taken with Nikon cameras and a wide variety of lenses, including zoom lenses. The preferred film of choice was Fujichrome slide films, which included Velvia, Provia and Sensia II.

Introduction

Kealakekua Bay, Big Island

Surrounded by warm, clear sub-tropical water, Hawaii attracts travelers from all parts of the globe who come to dive, snorkel and enjoy the shear beauty of this volcanic paradise. The Hawaiian islands offer great diversity above and below the clear Pacific Ocean and are a world-favorite vacation destination due to their extraordinary beauty and ease of travel. Hawaii is a melting pot of cultures wrapped up in a common theme of the Aloha spirit. Here you will find a friendly atmosphere and numerous activities. Whether it be climbing an active volcano or seeking a deserted beach for the day, or just about anything in-between, Hawaii has it all.

Divers and snorkelers will find that due to Hawaii's geographical isolation, geological youth and subtropical location, the bottom topography and marine life are very unique and different from most other dive destinations in the world. While you won't find the lush soft coral growth common in other tropical destinations such as Micro-

nesia, Fiji, or the Red Sea, Hawaii offers dramatic lava formations, fantastic visibility, and a chance to encounter larger marine life such as manta rays, turtles, and sharks. Travelers who visit in the winter months will also have a great opportunity to see humpback whales, along with dolphins and other cetaceans. Divers who slow down, take the time to learn about the marine life and look beyond the obvious will be able to identify an incredible abundance of endemic tropical fish species and colorful invertebrates that are found nowhere else in the world. Combine all this with

Hawaii's generally accommodating dive conditions and easily accessible dive sites and savvy divers agree that Hawaiian diving is truly world class. Since the last edition of this guide there have been changes in conservation efforts and the development of some new artificial reefs such as purposely sunken ships.

Organizations such as Hawaiian Islands Recreational Scuba Association (HIRSA), Malama Kai, Big Island Reef Fund, Maui Reef Fund and other industry groups have greatly improved the way Hawaii reefs are managed. In order to preserve this unique marine environment, general guidelines for anchoring and the use of boat moorings have been set. These efforts along with public awareness will allow the coral reefs to continue to be healthy and thrive. Additionally, Midway Island and Kahoolawe have been closed to the public and are no longer accessible.

This book is designed to provide divers and snorkelers with an overview of Hawaii's unique underwater world.

Throughout this diverse island chain, you'll find many conveniently located dive sites that are easy enough for newcomers to the sport, but still hold the interest of experienced dive enthusiasts. Many dive sites are remote and pristine, while others are current-swept and thrilling, often only suitable for advanced divers.

This guidebook covers four principal dive regions within the island chain: Oahu, Big Island (Hawaii), Maui County (including Maui, Molokini Crater, Lanai and Molokai), Kauai and Niihau. The dive sites described in this guide do not constitute a comprehensive list of all dive sites in Hawaii, but were selected as some of the best and most popular dives in their regions, and represent typical diving conditions in each area. Dive site descriptions include information to help you select dives suitable for your interests and abilities and to help establish a dive plan. Information on night diving, safe diving practices and underwater photography tips are interspersed throughout the text.

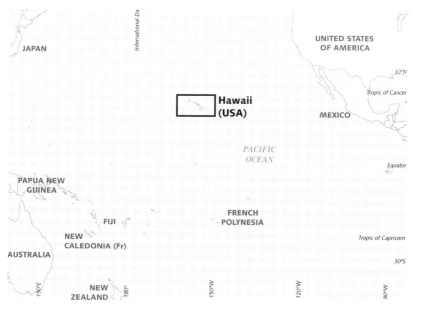

Mount Haleakala at sunrise, with the Big island in the background
photo: Andrew Sallmon

Facts about Hawaii

Volcanic in origin, most of the Hawaiian islands are high and rugged, cut by spectacular, lush green gorges and valleys. Their beaches range from beautiful, soft white sand to rough, dark lava rocks. The water is always warm and provides opportunities for virtually endless underwater exploration as well as world-class surfing, windsurfing and fishing.

Ethnically diverse Hawaii is an appealing collage of peoples and cultures. While less than 1% of the population is pure Hawaiian, almost a quarter of the islanders boast some Hawaiian ancestry, and there's a resurgence of interest in traditional Hawaiian culture among islanders of all races.

The Hawaiian islands' unique characteristics, mild climate, varied activities and cultural attributes have made them a favorite tourist destination, and tourism one of the state's biggest income generators.

GEOGRAPHY

Hawaii is the world's most isolated archipelago, resting more than 2400 miles (3864km) from the nearest land mass, North America. The Hawaiian archipelago is the northernmost extent of Polynesia and stretches across 1523 miles (2452km) of central Pacific Ocean from Kure Atoll in the northwest to the Big Island in the southeast. The eight major islands – Oahu, the Big Island, Maui, Kahoolawe, Lanai, Molokai, Kauai and Niihau – have a combined land mass of 6470 sq miles (16,757 sq km). The northwestern Hawaiian islands, which consist of 33 tiny atolls, are scattered across 1000 miles (1600km) of ocean north of Kauai.

Oahu is the gateway to the Hawaiian islands. Its beautiful beaches and mild climate have attracted vacationers since the early 1900s and Waikiki, just south of the capital city Honolulu, still accommodates nearly half of the state's visitors.

The largest and southernmost island is Hawaii, more commonly referred to as the 'Big Island' to avoid confusing it with the state as a whole. The Big Island is home to the state's highest mountain, Mauna Kea, which reaches 13,796ft (4139m) above sea level and is the world's highest mountain when measured from the ocean floor – 33,476ft (10,043m).

Maui County, north of Oahu, includes four islands and one crater – Maui, Kahoolawe, Lanai, Molokai and Molokini Crater. Maui, the most populated, is the jumping-off point for the region. The high volcanic mountains provide a stunning backdrop to waterfalls, scenic drives and lush green landscape. Kahoolawe is a small, uninhabited island southwest of Maui. Lanai is a fertile, teardrop-shaped island off Maui's northwest end. Molokai, just north of Lanai, is a rural, slow-paced island and home to the world's highest sea cliffs. Molokini Crater is the tip of an extinct volcano that rises out of the water between Maui and Kahoolawe. The shallow channels between these islands form a welcome breeding and calving ground for migratory humpback whales.

Farther north is Kauai, the 'Garden Island,' which is famous for its lush green vegetation and the jagged splendor of the Na Pali Coast. Just west of Kauai is Niihau, the 'Forbidden Island,' a low-lying, windswept island that is privately owned and inhabited solely by native Hawaiians.

Of the northwestern Hawaiian islands, Midway Island used to be the only one accessible to tourists. However, at the time of this writing it was no longer open to the public.

GEOLOGY

The Hawaiian islands are the tips of massive mountains, created by molten rock spewing out of a crack or hot spot in the earth's mantle for over 25 million years. While the hot spot is stationary, the ocean floor, which is part of the Pacific Plate, is moving northwest at the rate of about 3in (8cm) a year.

As weak spots in the earth's crust pass over the hot spot, molten lava bursts through and forms underwater volcanic mountains, some of which finally emerge above the water as islands. Each new volcano eventually creeps north from the hot spot that created it. The further the volcano is from the lava source, the lower the volcanic activity, until the volcano eventually becomes extinct.

Once volcanic activity stops, it's a downhill battle. The forces of erosion – wind, rain and waves – slowly wear away the mountains. In addition, the settling of the ocean floor causes the land to gradually recede. Thus the once-mountainous northwestern Hawaiian islands (the oldest in the Hawaiian chain) are now low, flat atolls that in time will be totally submerged. The Big Island, Hawaii's southernmost island, is still in the birthing process. Its most active volcano, Kilauea, is directly above the hot spot. The eruption of Kilauea began in 1983, and now in its 23rd year and 55th eruptive episode, ranks as the most voluminous outpouring of lava on the volcano's east rift zone in the past five centuries. By January 2005, 1.2 miles (2.7km) of lava had covered 72 miles (117km) and added 230 hectares

HAWAII'S GEOLOGICAL HISTORY

Less than 30 miles (48km) southeast of the Big Island, a new seamount named Loihi has already built up 15,000ft (4,500m) on the ocean floor. The growing mounds of lava are expected to break the ocean surface within 10,000 years; however, if it were to get hyperactive, it could emerge within a century or two.

Hawaii's volcanoes are shield volcanoes, which form not by explosion but by slowly building up layer upon layer of lava. They rise from the sea with gentle slopes and a relatively smooth surface. After eons of facing the elements, their surfaces become sharply eroded, as seen at the Na Pali cliffs on Kauai (the oldest of the main islands), the most jagged cliffs in Hawaii.

Hawaii's active volcanoes are Kilauea and Mauna Loa, both on the Big Island. The Big Island's Mauna Kea and Hualalai and Maui's Haleakala are dormant, but future eruptions are possible. The volcanoes on all the other Hawaiian islands are considered extinct.

Due to Hawaii's young geological age, most of the reefs are coastal fringing reefs generally found adjacent to the shore. This provides divers and snorkelers with easy access to many shallow areas with good visibility.

Around the older islands to the north are more-developed barrier reefs, which form as volcanic islands gradually erode and the coral around them builds up. Midway Island, which once had a much greater land mass and now has a barrier reef, is an example of this kind of reef development.

to Kilauea's southern shore, its flows destroying 189 structures and resurfacing 9 miles (14km) of highway with as much as 115ft (35m) of lava.

Octopus peeking above the reef

HISTORY

Though the Hawaiian islands are millions of years old, the first settlers arrived only 1500 years ago. These Polynesian settlers, believed to have sailed from the Marquesas Islands, lived harmoniously

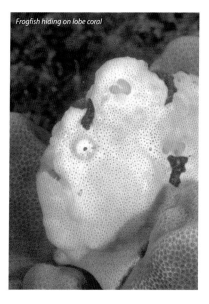
Frogfish hiding on lobe coral

British explorer Captain James Cook chanced upon the Hawaiian islands in 1778, after spending the better part of the decade exploring and charting the South Pacific. After a brief stay to restock provisions, Cook continued his northbound expedition.

Failing to find the fabled passage through the Arctic, he returned to Hawaii in 1779. When he sailed into the Big Island's beautiful **Kealakekua Bay** on January 17, he was greeted by thousands of canoes and generally treated like a god. His arrival coincided with the Makahiki Festival, a four-month-long event of games, festivities and peace dedicated to Lono, god of the harvest. Apparently, Cook was mistaken for this god.

When Cook returned a few weeks later to repair a broken mast, the Makahiki Festival had ended. Cook's timing and the conditions of his return proved inauspicious. A variety of misunderstandings and unfortunate events finally resulted in a group of native Hawaiians stabbing Cook to death. Cook's crew was able to safely return home with charts, drawings and stories of their travels. The western world would soon recognize the vast bounty of Hawaii.

until about 600 years ago when a new wave of more aggressive Tahitian immigrants arrived.

These newcomers soon conquered the initial, more passive residents and introduced a hierarchical social system that separated commoners from ruling chiefs and kings (called *alii* in Hawaiian). The conquerors also introduced human sacrifices to the gods and established the *kapu* system. *Kapu,* a complex code of behavior and social interaction, forbade commoners to eat the same food or even walk on the same ground as the *alii*. A commoner who crossed the shadow of a king could be put to death.

Kapu also prohibited women from eating bananas, coconuts, pork and some varieties of fish. One of the Tahitian immigrants, a powerful *kahuna* (Tahitian priest), erected the first *heiaus* (Hawaiian temples), some of which can still be seen today. These *heiaus* were generally dedicated to the god of the harvest, Lono, or the war god, Ku. It was in the *luakini heiaus* (the temples dedicated to Ku) that human sacrifices took place.

In 1819 the first missionaries and whaling ships arrived, both quickly flourishing. By 1855 the whaling industry had reached its peak, but the need for whale oil soon declined due to the increased use of petroleum oil. To compensate for this economic shift, Hawaii developed its agricultural industries.

As native Hawaiians were decimated by diseases introduced by migrants from Europe and the Americas, new labor forces were imported from China, Japan, the Philippines and Portugal, setting the foundation for a Hawaii that would be known as the cultural 'melting pot of the Pacific.'

The US annexed Hawaii in 1898, attracted not so much by its tropical climate as by its strategic location halfway

The Attack of Pearl Harbor

On December 7, 1941, a wave of Japanese bombers attacked Pearl Harbor, jolting the US into WWII. The attack caught the US fleet by surprise, and in the next few hours, 18 ships were sunk, more than 200 planes destroyed and at least 2500 lives were lost.

The USS *Arizona* was the single greatest loss, holding 1177 sailors when it took a direct hit, sinking in less than nine minutes.

between the US and its new possession, the Philippines. While Hawaii's economy boomed during the early 20th century as a result of the emerging sugar and pineapple industries, the US established military bases throughout the islands. Both Oahu and the Midway islands were used as operations bases and became integral defence points.

The US was jolted into WWII when a wave of Japanese bombers attacked Pearl Harbor on December 7, 1941. The US fleet was caught by surprise – more than 20 US ships and 347 aircraft were sunk, damaged or destroyed and 2500 people were killed.

Less than a year later, in June 1942, US troops retaliated by thwarting a Japanese surprise attack on Midway, stopping their further advancement into Pacific territories.

When Hawaii assumed US statehood in 1959, commercial development and urbanization intensified. Since that time, agricultural industries have all but vanished, and tourist enterprises have filled the economic gap. Tourism now represents the largest sector of Hawaii's economy, accounting for approximately 30% of the state's income.

Many tourists visit Hawaii to enjoy the island chain's unique marine life, and there are more than a hundred diving and snorkeling services catering to them.

ACTIVITIES & ATTRACTIONS

Hawaii's beautiful beaches and varied diving aren't the only aspects that have made it a tourist magnet. The islands offer a variety of activities suitable for the entire family or challenging enough for the most experienced adventurer, and there is something to fit all budgets. All beaches are public with no entrance fees, while resorts located on the beach are required to provide public access and free parking. There are no fees for state parks, including historical sites and other attractions located within the state parks. National parks, such as Hawaii Volcanoes National Park and Pu`uhonua o Honaunau National Historical Park on the Big Island, do charge entrance fees.

Following are some of the best and most popular activities and attractions throughout the islands. For a more comprehensive listing, see Lonely Planet's *Hawaii* travel guide.

OAHU

Oahu is world famous for its surfing and Waikiki Beach is where it all began. The surf conditions offer ample opportunities for beginners and rental boards and lessons are readily available. Another popular surf spot is just off Diamond Head, accessible via Diamond Head Road, where large south swells roll in during summer months. The surf can be viewed from several lookouts along the road. In winter months, Oahu's north shore turns into a surfer's heaven.

The waves can be huge and are definitely only suitable for experts. Here you'll find famous surf spots such as Banzai Pipeline, Sunset Beach and Waimea Bay.

On Oahu's north shore you'll find the Waimea Valley Adventure Park (just across the highway from Waimea Bay Beach Park) in the beautiful, lush Waimea Valley. This commercial operation boasts an array of fun activities, including horse riding, kayaking, mountain biking and ATV tours. To reach Waimea Falls, you can take the 0.8 mile (1.3km) long path that meanders through the botanical gardens or, if you prefer, you can take a short tram ride that winds its way to the waterfall.

Sea Life Park is just north of Makapuu Point on the windward side of Oahu's southeast tip. This large commercial affair boasts a huge 300,000 gallon (1,136,000L) tank displaying sharks, rays, moray eels and turtles. There is also an outdoor exhibit featuring several monk seals and two amphitheaters where dolphins and penguins perform their tricks.

The Waikiki Aquarium is the third oldest public museum in the US. Located on Waikiki Beach, this aquarium has more than 2,500 organisms representing in excess of 420 species of aquatic animals and plants. Of special interest are the shark, monk seal, nautilus and seahorse exhibits, displays of black-coral forests and rare endemic species that even divers seldom encounter.

The Bishop Museum in Honolulu is one of the Pacific's main natural-history museums and its collection features several compelling exhibits and galleries that document Polynesian and Melanesian cultures.

More than 1.5 million people remember Pearl Harbor each year with a visit to the USS *Arizona* Memorial. Operated by the National Park Service, the memorial is Hawaii's most visited attraction. The visitor center is open 7:30am to 5pm daily, except some holidays. Admission to the museum, the documentary film and the trip to the offshore memorial is free.

Day sailing boat on Waikiki Beach

BIG ISLAND

If you go to the Big Island, a visit to the Hawaii Volcanoes National Park is a must. The scenery is awesome, with dozens of craters and cinder cones. The centerpiece of the park is the steaming Kilauea Caldera (the sunken center of Kilauea Volcano), which is said to be the home of Pele, the Hawaiian goddess of volcanoes. Kilauea's southeast rift has been actively flowing since 1983. To obtain information on the volcano's current status and the best observation point to watch the lava flow, you can contact the park's 24-hour hotline at ☎ 808-985-6000. The caldera is about 2½ hours drive from Kailua-Kona (96 miles or 155km) or 40 minutes from Hilo (30 miles or 48km). It takes a further hour to get to where you can see lava flowing into the ocean, so be sure to allow ample time for the trip.

Mauna Kea's summit at 13,796ft (4139m) has some of the best stargazing conditions in the world. With its generally cloudless nights and clear, dry air, it's also no surprise the largest collection of state-of-the-art telescopes is assembled here. The visitor center offers free summit tours on weekends but you need your own transportation to reach the summit. Paradise Safaris runs guided tours at sunset that include transportation and stargazing with their own telescope.

In ancient Hawaiian times, commoners who broke a *kapu* (law) were hunted down and killed. Only those who were able to reach Puuhonua o Honaunau (Place of Refuge) before being captured were spared. Today, Place of Refuge is

Pimpled basket on lobe coral

a national historical park that contains ancient temples and other old Hawaiian buildings.

At 1 mile (1.6km) wide and nearly 6 miles (9.6km) deep, Waipio Valley is the largest of the seven dramatic amphitheater valleys on the windward side of the Kohala Mountains. The scenery here is spectacular, with cliffs that reach heights of up to 2000ft (600m) wrapping around the lush green valley which consists of tangled jungle vegetation, flower gardens, taro patches and stunning waterfalls. The narrow, steep road that winds down to Waipio is only accessible to hikers or four-wheel-drive vehicles. This spectacular valley is well worth visiting, and a variety of tours are available.

On the Big Island, whale watching is not just offered during humpback season: several charter operators run whale watching tours year-round. Although the humpbacks are the highlight of whale watching trips during the winter months, other whales – such as sperm whales and pilot whales – can be found in the deep waters further offshore.

The Big Island, with vast pasturelands and upcountry forests, has a rich ranching history and is also home to the largest privately owned ranch in the US. There are a variety of outfitters that offer horseback riding, with trail rides ranging from scenic mountain rides or explorations of the various ranches to trots through the spectacular Waipio Valley.

Some of the world's best deep-sea fishing is found along the Kona Coast, with Kona holding most of the world's records for Pacific blue marlin. Kona's shores drop off quickly into deep blue water, giving fast access to large game fish. The large lee provided by the Big Island's massive mountains extends several miles offshore and provides ideal fishing conditions. If you are interested in deep-sea fishing, you'll find dozens of fishing charter boats offering their services.

Molokini Crater from the air

MAUI COUNTY

Maui's Haleakala National Park is home to the world's largest dormant volcano, Haleakala. Its summit has long been considered a natural 'power point,' where magnetic and cosmic forces unite. Haleakala means 'house of the sun' in Hawaiian, and viewing the sunrise from the rim of the crater is considered a magical experience.

One way to enjoy this daily event is to sign up for a bicycling tour that begins at the summit before dawn. From there you'll enjoy a 38 mile (61km) ride downhill, dropping a total of 10,000ft (3000m) in elevation. Haleakala National Park also has an extensive network of spectacular hiking trails throughout its moonlike landscape. Before you start your adventure to Haleakala, be sure to check the weather forecast. Due to the elevation, it is often cloudy or rainy and the temperature tends to be significantly lower than along the coast.

The road to Hana is regarded by many as the most beautiful drive on earth. From Kahului, the road winds past spectacular scenery of gorgeous coastal views, emerald valleys, mountains and countless waterfalls and streams. Though the drive is only 50 miles (80km) long, it's not one to be rushed. The narrow highway leads you over 54 bridges and around more than 600 hairpin turns to finally bring you to the small community of Hana. Here, be sure to meet the friendly locals, or take a walk through the bamboo forest.

Each year, North Pacific humpback whales migrate from Alaska to the Hawaiian Islands. They spend each winter in Hawaii's warm waters, where they breed and bear their young. Since humpbacks like to stay in shallow water when they have newborn calves, the channels surrounding Maui tend to attract the largest numbers of whales, allowing for many outstanding whale watching opportunities. There are numerous charter operations that specialize in whale-watching cruises, but there are also some excellent shoreline whale-watching spots such as the stretches from Olowalu to Maalaea Bay, and Keawakapu Beach to Makena Beach. Divers often have the privilege of seeing whales during surface intervals, while cruising to the dive site or, on rare occasions, a humpback whale may be encountered during a dive.

Some of the world's best windsurfing spots are found on Maui. Hookipa Beach on the north shore is recognized as a world-class site for advanced windsurfers. Novice and intermediate windsurfers will find more suitable conditions at Spreckelsville Beach or Kanaha Beach in Kahului Bay. There are numerous shops in Kahului that rent windsurfing boards and offer lessons.

The Maui Ocean Center in Wailuku is a state-of-the-art aquarium featuring a 600,000 gallon (2,730,000 liter) tank that is home to tiger sharks, rays and other big fish. Marine life enthusiasts will enjoy both the indoor and outdoor displays, which introduce the Hawaiian underwater world through coral reef scenes, lava formation exhibits and deep-sea creatures. Of special interest to divers are the tanks with frogfish and garden eels, critters that are normally either well camouflaged or concealed within the reef's crevices. Visitors also learn about the Hawaiian culture and its age-old link to the sea.

7-11 crabs are often seen in the lava tubes and caverns

KAUAI & NIIHAU

Kayaking has become one of the most popular ways to explore some of Kauai's most remote coastal wilderness areas, such as the dramatic Na Pali Coast and otherwise inaccessible parts of the Huleia, Wailua and Hanalei Rivers.

A variety of kayak outfitters rent kayaks and offer guided tours. The advantages of a guided tour include increased safety, access to restricted natural areas and management of difficult logistics. Some operators include famous attractions such as the movie sites of Raiders of the Lost Ark in their guided excursions, while others specialize in honeymoon packages. Kayak Kauai is best known for an adventurous tour along the Na Pali cliffs.

If you are looking for a less active (but just as exhilarating) means to explore the Na Pali Coast, you can join an ocean Zodiac safari or take a helicopter ride to marvel at the sheer cliffs and cascading waterfalls from a bird's-eye view. Any of these adventure tours will provide you with an unforgettable experience and spectacular scenery found only on Kauai.

Other ways to explore Kauai's awesome wilderness are on horseback or four-wheel-drive tours. CJM Country Stables offers rides to secluded beaches along the southwest shore, while Princeville Ranch Stables guides riders through north Kauai's lush valleys. Kauai Mountain Tours offers a beautiful and informative four-wheel-drive mountain tour.

Often referred to as the 'Grand Canyon of the Pacific', Waimea Canyon was created over the course of millions of years by the waters that drain from Mount Waialeale, whose summit has been called the wettest spot on earth.

by the Robinson family since 1864. Inhabited solely by native Hawaiians, the island has been entirely closed to tourism until recent years, when the family began to allow a limited number of tourists to visit and view the island via helicopter tours from Kauai. While you can join a three-hour tour to a remote beach, you are not likely to catch even a glimpse of a Hawaiian settlement or any of the 200 residents. If the idea of hunting Polynesian boar and wild sheep appeals to you, Niihau Safaris also offers hunting trips to the outer reaches of Niihau.

It receives an estimated 480in (1219cm) of precipitation each year. The 2785ft-(836m-) deep canyon provides amazing scenery, regardless of whether you go on an extended hike into the canyon, take a walk along one of the marked trails or simply drive to one of the scenic lookouts.

Bird-watching can be a rewarding experience at any of the wildlife refuges, which are home to migratory seabirds and non-migratory endemic fowl.

In the Hanalei and Huleia National Wildlife refuges you can see endangered native species such as the Hawaiian duck, Hawaiian coot and Hawaiian stilt. Kilauea Point National Park is an excellent area to observe tropical birds, great frigates, shearwaters and other seabirds.

You can also venture to Kauai's neighboring island Niihau, the 'Forbidden Island,' which has been privately owned

Hawaiian monk seals (Monachus schauinslandi) are commonly found on the sandy beaches and surrounding waters of the northwestern Hawaiian archipelago, but have been seen more frequently throughout the Hawaiian islands in recent years. Females can reach a length of 7.5ft (2.3m) and weigh up to 600lbs (273kg). Males are a little smaller, reaching 6.8ft (2.1m) and weighing more than 500lbs (230kg). Adults have a silver-gray back fading to a cream-colored belly, though both back and belly darken with age.

During the 19th century, Hawaiian monk seals were exploited by hunters. They are now endangered and protected under the US Endangered Species Act. The current population of 1300 to 1400 animals is still at risk, threatened by ingestion of harmful substances, a decrease in food availability, intentional kills and incidental capture. Natural factors such as an inherently slow reproductive rate have made it difficult for the population to stabilize and re-establish itself. The protection of critical habitat and mitigation of human disturbance are critical conservation and protection strategies.

The rare and endemic Hawaiian longfin anthias can
sometimes be found on patch reefs at depth

Diving in Hawaii

Harlequin shrimp can be seen on dusk and night dives

Diving in Hawaii is generally favourable all year round, especially on the leeward side of the islands. Divers can look forward to incredible lava caves, arches and other underwater formations, along with a variety of wrecks and pristine hard-coral gardens. The many small, isolated bays make for great snorkeling adventures and excellent shore diving when the weather is calm. Divers and snorkelers who venture out on one of the many day excursions often enjoy dolphins playing in the boat's wake. December through April is the humpback whale season, which often features outstanding surface displays by these incredible creatures.

The underwater topography in Hawaii is made up of lava tubes, archways and finger reefs. Many diving and snorkeling sites are located directly offshore but, due to a variety of factors, are only safely accessible by boat. Boat dives allow you to see the best the islands have to offer while providing a safer, more relaxing and fun experience. Boats vary in size and capacity: some take up to six, others 12 and in some cases 24 or more passengers. Generally, dive operators will provide enough divemasters to split divers into groups of six or less. Some operators cater to specific nationalities of divers (evident by brochures and advertising in many languages), though most are multilingual.

Live-aboard enthusiasts will find two vessels which operate along the Kona and Kohala Coasts of the Big Island. The Kona Aggressor II is based in Kailua-Kona, accommodates up to 14 passengers and generally runs one-week charters. The Sunseeker operates out of Honokahau Harbor and caters to a maximum of six divers. Charter length and schedules vary based on divers' requests. See the Listings section for details.

Shore diving opportunities vary from island to island and day to day. Though shore diving in Hawaii is practiced regularly by locals, it is wise to learn the local conditions before attempting any of these dives. One way to ensure you select the safest shore dives, with respect to current weather conditions is to hire a local dive guide. Those on a tight budget may want to dive the popular shore diving areas on the weekend in order to watch local divers enter the water (often a tricky task on Hawaii's rocky coastlines) and perhaps ask a few questions. Be sure to stop by a local dive shop for professional advice and guidance. Some dive operators organize local shore dives guided by a professional divemaster. This combines safety with specific information about each site's unique highlights at a price that generally suits even budget-oriented divers. An experienced guide can also point out critters often overlooked by most divers.

Hawaii also has a number of active local dive clubs, underwater photo competitions and scheduled underwater clean-up efforts.

Snuba Diving

Snuba is a fun and easy way to explore Hawaii's underwater world

Designed as an introduction to diving, snuba is a hybrid of diving and snorkeling. Snuba divers breathe compressed air like a scuba diver, but the air is supplied via a regulator and a 20ft- to 40ft- (6m- to 12m-) long hose connected to an air tank which floats in a raft on the surface of the water. A small harness keeps the regulator in place.

Without the heavy and technical equipment normally associated with diving, snuba is far less intimidating than a 'real' dive. Snuba makes underwater exploration easier than either snorkeling or free-diving since you don't have to hold your breath or constantly return to the surface for air. Even children as young as eight years old can do this with only a little training, and a lot of success. There are, however, a few disadvantages: snuba depths are limited by the length of the hose, and snuba diving can't be safely performed in areas with lava formations, currents, wrecks or anywhere else where the hoses could get tangled.

WHAT TO BRING

General Supplies

A casual attitude toward dress prevails. Shorts, sandals and a T-shirt are standard throughout the islands. An Aloha shirt (a colorful Hawaiian-print shirt) with lightweight slacks for men and a cotton dress for women are sufficiently dressy even for formal occasions. If you plan to travel to higher elevations, be sure to bring a sweater and raincoat. Good walking shoes are also recommended for visits to rocky or mountainous areas such as Hawaii Volcanoes National Park.

As in most western countries, you'll find everything you need on Hawaii's five main islands, though at a 25% higher cost than on the US mainland. Outer islands such as Molokai and Lanai have a limited stock of retail goods, so consider bringing your own film, batteries or other items you are particular about. Though pharmacies on the main islands are readily available and well stocked, it is a good idea to bring a supply of any prescription medicine you require to last for the duration of your trip.

Snorkeler observing moorish idols

Dive-Related Equipment

Hawaii's five main islands are well stocked with quality rental and retail equipment. Most dive operators only rent 3mm shorty wetsuits. If you are visiting in winter, when water temperatures can drop below 74°F (23°C), and you tend to get cold easily or plan to dive a lot, bring your own 5mm wetsuit. Not all dive shops sell 5mm suits, so if you plan to purchase a warmer wetsuit when you arrive, call ahead to ensure there is one available.

Underwater Photography

The growing popularity of digital photography has extended to the underwater world. More and more underwater photographers, amateur and professional, are trading in their film cameras for digital technology and many diver operations are offering digital rental cameras. If you are looking to rent a camera, avoid disappointment and reserve one ahead. Photographers shooting on film will find it increasingly difficult to find developing services. At the time of this writing E-6 processing was still available on the more populated islands of Oahu and Maui. On Oahu, E-6 processing is available at retail stores such as Fox Photo, Light Ink and Fromes. On Maui, labs offering fast E-6 processing services, include Maui Custom Color Lab, Fox Photo and others. However, if this is an essential serv-

The unique underwater terrain formed by volcanic activity adds interest to nearly all of Hawaii's dive sites. Lava ridges and fingers often lay the base for coral reefs, while lava caves, caverns, tunnels and archways are awesome to explore. Lava tends to be porous and covered with small nooks and crannies (called *pukas* in Hawaiian) that underwater critters convert into homes. Areas of relatively young lava activity – huge flows of coal-black lava where coral has not yet established itself – are dramatic seascapes in their own right.

Lava continues to flow into the sea every day from the still-active Kilauea Volcano on the Big Island. Many divers inquire about diving where the red-hot lava meets the ocean. Although technically possible, it is not recommended. Diving in the vicinity of volcanic activity is dangerous, the water temperature extremely hot and burns are almost inevitable. Underwater explosions and lava avalanches are quite common when the glowing lava and the cool salt water mix, and constitute additional dangers that divers are better off avoiding.

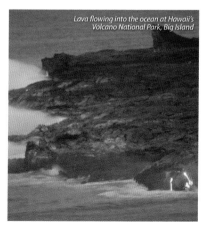

Lava flowing into the ocean at Hawaii's Volcano National Park, Big Island

Magic Island (Oahu)
Inside Reef (Oahu)
Three Tables (Oahu)
Kaiwi Point (Big Island)
Kahalu (Big Island)
Kealakekua Bay (Big Island)
Place of Refuge (Big Island)
Black Rock (Maui)
Inside Crater (Maui)
Kee Lagoon (Kauai)

Instructor explaining the proper use of the dive equipment

ice you will need, it is recommended that you check in advance to ensure it is still available.

DIVE TRAINING & CERTIFICATION

If you have never dived before, Hawaii is the perfect place to start. The clear tropical water and colorful shallow reefs are forgiving for first-time divers. Recent changes to entry-level diving requirements have made learning to dive easier than ever before, without compromising safety. Just about anyone with reasonably good health can venture underwater. Whether you want to try diving for the first time or undertake advanced certification, there's likely to be a program that meets your needs and goals.

Some organizations offer pool-only scuba programs for children between eight and 11 years old. For people aged 12 and up, beginner programs such as the popular 'resort course' start you out in either a pool or calm, shallow ocean site. Upon successful completion of the confined water session, beginners are qualified to dive with a professional instructor for the duration of their holiday. The dives and any of the accomplished skills may be credited toward an Open Water certification (as long as your certification is completed within 12 months). The specifics of these programs can vary, so inquire before signing up.

Full certification classes are available for those with varying budgets and time constraints. If you have only a few days, you may need to sign up for a one-on-one class with an instructor who can modify the course to fit your schedule. Generally, a minimum of four days is required.

If a limited budget is more of an issue than time, you can join a class designed for residents. These classes are generally held in the evening or on weekends over the course of a few weeks or months. The cost may be as low as $100, but varies with the number of students enrolled and if materials or boat dives are included.

Diver peering into lava tube

The dive sites in this book are rated according to the following diver skill-level rating system. These are not absolute ratings but apply to divers at a particular time, diving at a particular place. For instance, someone unfamiliar with prevailing conditions might be considered a novice diver at one dive area, but an intermediate diver at another, more familiar location.

Novice
A novice diver should be accompanied by an instructor, divemaster or advanced diver on all dives. A novice diver generally fits the following profile:
- holds basic scuba certification from an internationally recognized certifying agency
- dives infrequently (less than one trip a year)
- logged fewer than 25 total dives
- little or no experience diving in similar waters and conditions
- dives no deeper than 60ft (18m)

Intermediate
An intermediate diver generally fits the following profile:
- may have participated in some form of continuing diver education
- logged between 25 and 100 dives
- dives no deeper than 130ft (40m)
- has been diving in similar waters and conditions within the last six months

Advanced
An advanced diver generally fits the following profile:
- advanced certification
- has been diving for more than two years and logged more than 100 dives
- has been diving in similar waters and conditions within the last six months.

Regardless of skill level, you should be in good physical condition and know your limitations. If uncertain of your own level of expertise for a particular site, ask the advice of a local dive instructor. He or she is best qualified to assess your abilities based on the site's prevailing dive conditions. Ultimately, however, you must decide if you are capable of making a particular dive, a decision that should take into account your level of training, recent experience and physical condition, as well as the conditions at the site. Remember that conditions can change at any time, even during a dive.

Close encounters with friendly fish are common while snorkeling Hawaii's calm shallow bays

There are many options that fall between the more expensive but fast private lessons and the inexpensive but lengthy group classes. Options vary between dive operators and prices often hinge on the number of students in the class.

Another popular option is the Open Water referral program, where pool and classroom sessions are completed at a dive shop near home, and the open water or check-out dives are conducted while vacationing in Hawaii. There are some restrictions and time limits, so be sure to get specific information from both your local dive shop and the Hawaiian operator well ahead of time.

Certified divers will find that many of the dive shops on the main islands offer a wide range of specialty classes, including various technical diving courses. Call ahead for class schedules and requirements for the courses you're interested in.

SNORKELING

Many of Hawaii's dive sites – particularly the shallow, sheltered bays – are just as rewarding and enjoyable for snorkelers as they are for divers.

Snorkeling is certainly the easiest, and generally the least expensive, way to enjoy the underwater world. You only need a mask, snorkel and fins, though additional items may be desirable. Flotation devices such as an inflatable vest, an inner tube or a kickboard can enhance the experience. A long-sleeved T-shirt or lycra skin will help prevent sunburn, while rubber-soled booties are essential in areas that involve walking over sharp lava rocks to reach snorkeling entry locations.

Pyramid butterflyfish are commonly found with black coral

If you plan to snorkel from shore, it is advisable to hire a local guide or stay in areas under the supervision of a lifeguard. Be sure to inquire about prevailing currents and other possible hazards, then evaluate your physical abilities against the conditions. Shore entry and snorkeling near shore can be complicated by waves and currents. A good rule to remember is to never turn your back to the ocean. Waves can take you by surprise if you are not alert. They generally come in sets, so if one passes, another is likely to be close behind.

Joining a boat cruise is usually the safest snorkeling option. On all major islands you'll find many businesses offer half-day snorkeling tours that generally include snorkeling instruction, equipment, additional flotation devices, freshwater showers, snacks and/or lunch. This is a great way to spend a day.

DIVE OPERATORS

There are many dive operators in Hawaii – some in large dive centres, others who work out of the back of their cars, and many in-between. Since diving requires thorough training and uncompromised safety, it is important to find a responsible operator.

Ask around about any operator you may be considering. Often you can gather information from friends or via the internet. Your questions should cover, but not be limited to, the type of rental equipment used, make of the boat and how many divers it carries, the ratio of divers to dive guides, the cost of diving, the level of certification of dive guides, the trips schedule etc. Generally, any operation that offers boat trips is usually a legitimate operator. Hawaii watersports businesses are subject to many state laws and Federal Coast Guard regulations. This alone generally weeds out fly-by-night operators. However, it's always good practice to do a bit of background research.

Endangered monk seal enjoys a nap on a sandy beach

Diving Conservation & Awareness

Humpback whales breed and calf while in Hawaiian waters during the winter months
photo: Andrew Sallmon

During the last few decades it has begun to dawn on humans world wide that we need to be proactive in regards to protecting our natural resources, and Hawaii is no exception. Hawaiian reefs and the surrounding marine life are threatened by many factors, which include pollution, runoff from agricultural regions and golf courses, overfishing and the collection of aquarium fish. The good news is, this is where the biggest changes in the Hawaiian dive industry have occurred over the past few years. Conservation groups have worked through legislative action to set aside Marine Conservation Districts (MCD) and Fisheries Management Areas (FMA) in order to protect the island chain's precious underwater resources. These organizations have been instrumental in the installation of day-use mooring buoys, providing public education and outreach, marine science education and research, and community-based management of coastal and marine resources.

Visiting divers can make a tax deductible donation to these not-for-profit groups, in addition to participating in local activities. Ask about current activities at the local dive shops when you arrive or check the websites of Hawaii's conservation groups for more information.

MARINE RESERVES & REGULATIONS

In areas referred to as FMAs (Fisheries Management Areas) or MLCDs (Marine Life Conservation Districts), fish collecting, fish feeding and spearfishing are not permitted, or are at least restricted. Though the two are very similar, FMAs tend to be less strict and to focus on protecting fish by regulating collection and fishing. Fish feeding may not be regulated and coral is generally not protected. There are numerous FMAs throughout the islands, usually located in non-diving areas such as harbors, wharves and freshwater spots.

The following regions are designated MLCDs: Hanauma Bay (Oahu); Pupukea (Oahu), covering the dive sites **Three Tables** and **Shark's Cove**; Waikiki Beach (Oahu), near Diamond Head; **Kealakekua Bay** (Big Island); Lapakahi (Big Island), along the north Kohala

Coast; Waialea Bay (Big Island), on the south Kohala Coast; Old Kona Airport (Big Island); Molokini Crater (Maui); Honolua-Mokuleia Bay (Maui), along the northwestern coast; and Manele-Hulopoe Bay, near the Manele Boat Harbor (Lanai).

Certain species are specifically protected by law, including the green sea turtles. You can be fined for touching, feeding or otherwise bothering them. The Hawaiian islands have been designated a National Marine Sanctuary to protect the winter breeding and calving grounds of the endangered North Pacific humpback whale. Boats, divers and snorkelers are forbidden to approach these whales closer than 300ft (90m).

Conservation efforts continue with the creation and expansion of protected areas. Recently, a bill was passed to protect approximately 30% of the Kona and Kohala coastlines from fish collecting and fishing. These areas are known as Fish Replenishment Areas (FRA). However, at the time of this writing there were two bills in the Hawaii legislature that would effectively overturn many of these conservation laws. In addition, enforcement remains one of the greatest challenges facing all protected areas due to the under-resourced and under-staffed enforcement agencies' inability to effectively patrol protected areas.

RESPONSIBLE DIVING

Dive sites are located where the reefs and walls display the most beautiful corals and sponges. It only takes a moment – an inadvertently placed hand or knee, or a careless brush or kick with a fin – to destroy this fragile and delicate living ecosystem. By following certain basic guidelines while diving, you can help preserve the ecology and beauty of the reefs:

1   Never drop boat anchors onto a coral reef and take care not to ground boats on coral. Always encourage dive operators and regulatory bod-

Racoon butterflyfish commonly school on Hawaiian reefs

ies in their efforts to establish permanent moorings at appropriate dive sites.

2 Practice and maintain proper buoyancy control and avoid over-weighting. Be aware buoyancy can change during an extended trip. Initially you may breathe harder and need more weighting; a few days later you may breathe more easily and require less weight. Tip: Use your weight belt and tank position to maintain a horizontal position – raise them to elevate your feet, lower to elevate your upper body. Also, pay attention to buoyancy loss: as you go deeper, your wetsuit compresses, as does the air in your BC.

3 Avoid touching living marine organisms with your body and equipment. Polyps can be damaged by even the gentlest contact. Never stand on or touch living coral. The use of gloves is no longer recommended: gloves make it too easy to hold on to the reef. The abrasion caused by gloves may be even more damaging to the reef than your hands are. If you must hold on to the reef, touch only exposed rock or dead coral.

4 Take great care in underwater caves. Spend as little time within them as possible, as your air bubbles can damage fragile organisms. Divers should take turns inspecting the interiors of small caves or under ledges to lessen the chances of damaging contact.

5 Be conscious of your fins. Even without contact, the surge from heavy fin strokes near the reef can do damage. Avoid full-leg kicks when diving close to the bottom and when leaving a photo scene. When you inadvertently kick something, stop kicking! (It seems obvious, but some divers either panic or remain totally oblivious when they bump something.) When treading water in shallow reef areas, take care not to kick up clouds of sand. Settling sand can smother the delicate reef organisms.

6 Secure gauges, computer consoles and your octopus regulator so they don't dangle – they are like miniature wrecking balls to a reef.

7 When swimming in strong currents, be extra careful in regard to leg kicks and handholds.

8 Photographers need to take extra precautions as cameras and equipment affect buoyancy. Changing f-stops, framing a subject and maintaining position for a photo often conspire to prohibit the ideal 'no-touch' approach on a reef. When you must use 'holdfasts,' choose them intelligently (ie, use one finger only for leverage off an area of dead coral).

9 Resist the temptation to collect or buy coral or shells. Aside from the ecological damage, taking home marine souvenirs depletes the beauty of a site and spoils other divers' enjoyment.

10 Take home all your trash and any litter you may find as well. Plastics in particular pose a serious threat to marine life.

11 Resist the temptation to feed fish. You may disturb their normal eating habits, encourage aggressive behaviour or feed them food that is detrimental to their health.

12 Minimize your disturbance of marine animals. Don't ride on the backs of turtles or manta rays as this can cause them great anxiety.

Health & Safety

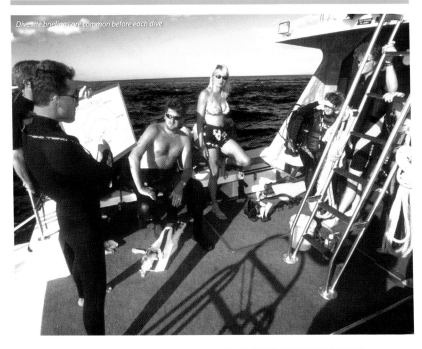
Dive site briefings are common before each dive

GENERAL HEALTH

There are few serious health issues to be concerned with in Hawaii, which is fortunately free of tropical diseases such as malaria, yellow fever and cholera. No immunizations are required to enter Hawaii or any other state in the US.

Generally, Hawaii provides some of the world's safest diving conditions, but when it's surgy, sharp and unforgiving lava rocks present a potential hazard to divers. Always stay alert for changing conditions, whether you are entering the water or already underwater.

The most notable health risks are sun overexposure, dehydration and heat exhaustion which can be easily prevented by using sunblock and protective clothing, choosing dive boats that provide a shaded area, drinking plenty of fluids, and slowing down to 'Hawaiian time.'

PRE-TRIP PREPARATION

General state of health, diving skill level and specific equipment needs are the three most important factors that impact on any dive trip. If you honestly assess these before you leave, you'll be well on your way to assuring a safe dive trip.

Firstly, if you're not in shape, start exercising. Secondly, if you haven't dived for a while (six months is too long) and your skills are rusty, do a local dive with an experienced buddy or take a scuba review course. Finally, inspect your dive gear. Feeling good physically, diving with experience and diving with reliable equipment not only increases your safety, but will also enhance your enjoyment underwater.

Inspect your dive gear at least a month before your trip. Remember, your regulator should be serviced annually, whether you've used it or not. If you use a dive computer and can replace the battery yourself, change it before the trip or buy a spare one to take along. Otherwise, send the computer to the manufacturer for a battery replacement.

If possible, find out if the dive center rents or services the type of gear you own. If not, you might want to take spare parts or even spare gear. An extra mask is always a good idea.

Purchase any additional equipment you might need, such as a dive light and tank marker light for night diving, a line reel for wreck diving etc. Make sure you have at least a whistle attached to your BC. Better yet, add a marker tube (also known as a safety sausage or come-to-me).

About a week before taking off, do a final check of your gear, grease o-rings, check batteries and assemble a save-a-dive kit. This kit should at minimum contain extra mask and fin straps, snorkel keeper, mouthpiece, valve cap, zip ties and o-rings.

Don't forget to pack a first-aid kit and medications such as decongestants, ear drops, antihistamines and seasickness tablets.

SIGNALING DEVICES

Occasionally a diver becomes lost or is left behind at a dive site – make sure this never happens to you!

A diver is extremely difficult to locate in the water, so always dive with a signaling device of some sort, preferably more than one.

One of the best signaling devices and the easiest to carry is a whistle. Even the little ones are extremely effective. Use a zip tie to attach one permanently to your BC. Even better, though more expensive, is a loud airhorn that connects to the inflator hose. You simply push a button to let out a blast. It does require

air from your tank to function, though. In order to be seen as well as heard, you should also carry a marker tube. The best ones are bright in color and about 6ft to 10ft (2m to 3m) high. They roll up and can easily fit into a BC pocket or can clip onto a D-ring. These can be inflated both orally or with a regulator. Some allow you to insert a dive light into the tube – a nice feature when it's dark.

Recompression & Medical Facilities

Hawaii has two recompression facilities equipped to treat dive-related decompression injuries, both on Oahu. In a dive emergency call ☎ 911, the Coast Guard or DAN. Each of these contacts can assess the situation and arrange for appropriate transportation to the nearest suitable facility. In such an emergency, don't contact or drive to a medical center directly, as it may not be able to treat your condition.

Hawaii has 25 acute-care hospitals. While the rural islands of Molokai and Lanai have limited medical facilities, the other main islands have fully staffed and modern hospitals. Call ☎ 911 from any island to contact the nearest emergency facility.

Diving & Flying

Most divers in Hawaii arrive and depart by air. While it's fine to dive soon after flying, it's important to remember that your last dive should be completed at least 12 hours (some experts advise 24 hours, particularly after repetitive dives) before your flight in order to minimize the risk of decompression sickness, caused by residual nitrogen in the blood. Keep in mind that this recommendation has changed and you may want to check with the local shop or on the internet to get the current guidelines.

Clear water and good visibility are common in Hawaii

Other signaling aides include mirrors, flares and dye markers, but these have limited reliability. A simple dive light is particularly versatile. Not only can it be used during the day for looking into crevices and crannies, it also comes in handy for nighttime signaling. Some even have a special strobe feature. Whenever you're diving, consider carrying at least a small light.

DAN

Divers Alert Network (DAN) is an international membership association of individuals and organizations sharing a common interest in diving and safety. It operates a 24-hour diving emergency hotline in the US: ☎ 919-684-8111 or ☎ 919-684-4DAN (4326). The latter accepts collect calls in a dive emergency. Though DAN does not directly provide medical care, it does provide advice on early treatment, evacuation and hyperbaric treatment of diving-related injuries. Divers should contact DAN for assistance as soon as a diving emergency is suspected.

DAN membership is reasonably priced and includes DAN TravelAssist, a membership benefit that covers medical air evacuation from anywhere in the world for any illness or injury. For a small additional fee, divers can get secondary insurance coverage for decompression sickness. For membership questions, contact DAN on ☎ 800-446-2671 within the US or on ☎ 919-684-2948 from elsewhere, or refer to the website (www.diversalertnetwork.org).

Schooling goatfish

All Emergencies:
US Emergency Operator; ☎ 911

Dive-Related Emergencies:
US Coast Guard Rescue Coordination Center; ☎ 541-2500
Divers Alert Network (DAN);
☎ 919-684-4326

General Medical Care:
Oahu
Queen's Medical Center; ☎ 538-9011
Big Island Kona Hospital; ☎ 322-9311
Hilo Hospital; ☎ 974-4700
Maui
Maui Memorial Hospital; ☎ 244-9056
Lanai Lanai Community Hospital;
☎ 565-6411
Kauai
Wilcox Memorial Hospital; ☎ 245-1100

Diver hovering above black coral

Oahu

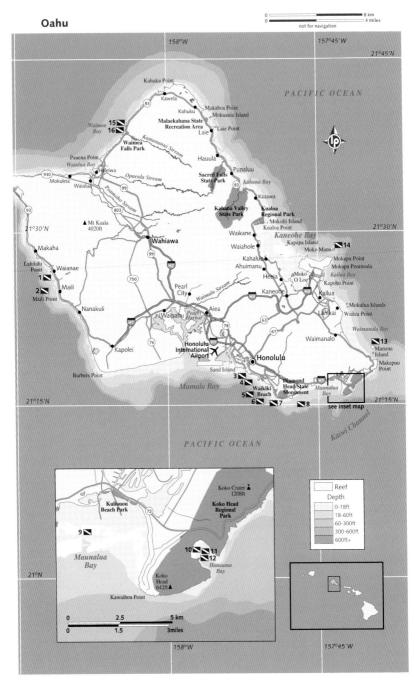

0 ————— 8 km
0 ————— 4 miles
not for navigation

158°W

157°45'W

21°45'N

PACIFIC OCEAN

Kahuku Point
Kawela
Makaboa Point
Kahuku
Mokuauia Island
Waimea **15**
Bay **16**
Malaekahana State
Recreation Area
Laie Point
Waimea
Falls Park
Laie
Kamananui Stream
Hauula
Pauena Point
Waialua Bay
Haleiwa
Mokuleia
930
Waialua
Opaeula Stream
Sacred Falls
State Park
Punaluu
Kahana Bay
99
803
Poamoha Stream
Kahana Valley
State Park
Kaaawa
93
Kualoa
Regional Park
Mokolii Island
Kualoa Point

21°30'N
▲ Mt Kaala
4020ft
Wahiawa
Waikane
Kaneohe Bay
21°30'N
Kapapa Island
Moko Manu **14**
99
H2
Waiahole
Makaha
Waikane
Kahaluu
Mokapu Point
Lahilahi
Point
1
Waianae
750
Ahuimanu
Mokapu Peninsula
Kailua Bay
Maili
2
Pearl
City
Waimalu Stream
Heeia
Moko
O Loe
Kapoho Point
Maili Point
H1
H3
Kaneohe
88
Kailua
Nanakuli
Waipahu
Pearl
Harbor
Aiea
Mokulua Islands
Wailea Point
76
78
Lanikai
63
Kapolei
Honolulu
International
Airport
61
Waimanalo
Waimanalo Bay
13
Barbers Point
Honolulu
Sand Island
*Manana
Island*
Makapuu
Point
3
4
Diamond
Head State
Monument
Mamala Bay
Waikiki
Beach
*Maunalua
Bay*
5
see inset map
21°15'N
6 **7** **8**
21°15'N

Kaiwi Channel

PACIFIC OCEAN

Koko Crater ▲
1208ft
Kuliouou
Beach Park
72
Koko Head
Regional
Park
9
*Maunalua
Bay*
10 **11**
12
*Hanauma
Bay*
21°N
Koko
Head
642ft ▲
Kawaihoa Point

0 ——— 2.5 ——— 5 km
0 ——— 1.5 ——— 3miles

☐ Reef
Depth
0-18ft
18-60ft
60-300ft
300-600ft
600ft+

158°W
157°45'W

Oahu Dive Sites

A rare daytime sighting of a Spanish dancer nudibranch

By far the most developed of the islands, Oahu has a culturally and ethnically diverse population of close to a million people. This melting pot offers all the excitement of a large cosmopolitan area alongside the pleasures of a tropical island: nightlife, fine dining and interesting museums complementing great beaches, surfing and good diving and snorkeling.

Oahu is the only island that offers several first-class wreck dives, which continue to get better as their marine life populations increase. Although Oahu's reefs do not generally have the pristine coral and superb visibility found on most of the other islands, there is a nice balance of reef and volcanic cavern dives with swirling, colorful fish. Several shallow reefs also make excellent shore dives for both divers and snorkelers.

As both the most populated and most visited Hawaiian island, Oahu has the greatest number of dive operators and dive shops, the majority of which are modern and up-to-date. Equipment rentals and airfills are readily available around the island. Some shops specialize in teaching courses designed for locals and the military, while others cater mostly to visitors.

Dive sites on Oahu are divided into four main regions: the leeward side, the south coast (including Hanauma Bay), the windward side and the north shore.

LEEWARD SIDE

Oahu's sheltered leeward side, extending from Kaena Point to Diamond Head, is one of the state's most popular diving areas, thanks to nearly year-round accessibility. Several wrecks that shelter a variety of fish and coral species from the strong currents that often flow through the area, while lava formations provide additional places to look for interesting marine life.

Oahu Dive Sites	GOOD SNORKELING	NOVICE	INTERMEDIATE	ADVANCED
1 MAKAHA CAVERNS	•	•		
2 THE MAHI			•	
3 KEWALO PIPES			•	
4 MAGIC ISLAND	•	•		
5 YO-257			•	
6 THE SEA TIGER WRECK				•
7 THE BABY BARGE			•	
8 CORSAIR				•
9 TURTLE CANYON	•	•		
10 INSIDE REEF	•	•		
11 OUTSIDE REEF	•		•	
12 WITCH'S BREW				•
13 MANANA ISLAND				•
14 MOKU MANU				•
15 SHARK'S COVE	•	•		
16 THREE TABLES	•		•	

Diver entering lava tubes at Makaha Caverns

1 MAKAHA CAVERNS

Location: *West of Waianae Boat Harbor*
Depth Range: *20-45ft (6-14m)*
Access: *Boat or Shore*
Expertise Rating: *Intermediate*

Makaha Caverns is an interesting shallow site that can be mind-blowing when the visibility is good. Normal visibility is 50ft to 60ft, though it can be as much as 100ft when the seas are calm and there has been little rain or run off to cloud the water.

Two large open-ended lava tubes form a V-shaped cavern found about a hundred yards from shore. Near the openings you can expect to see large schools of bluestripe snappers and yellowstripe goatfish. The tubes are easy to swim through, and with the help of a flashlight, you'll discover several dense schools of soldierfish, along with Hawaiian bigeyes and squirrelfish.

The large rubble area surrounding the cavern is worth checking for octopuses, devil scorpionfish and juvenile dragon wrasses. With a little luck, you may even see mantas and green sea turtles in the vicinity.

If you like to combine night diving with the comfort of boat diving, this is your spot. It's shallow, easy diving with little current (though occasionally it can be surgy) and has an abundance of nocturnal life.

The critters that hide inside during the daytime – such as reef crabs, spiny lobsters, colorful reef shrimp and Spanish dancers – come out onto the open reef to feed. It is not recommended to enter the cavern at night, even when conditions are calm. It may be disorienting since it's too dark to clearly see the exit, and in any case, the creatures are all out on the reef.

Though entering the wreck is not advised due to its collapsed state, you will find that with the aid of a flashlight there are many soldierfish, squirrelfish, spiny lobsters and crabs, along with other invertebrates that live inside the interior of the wreck. Most of the marine life is found outside the wreck, upon which an abundance of sponges and corals have established themselves over the years. Lovely snowflake and tubastrea (cup) corals decorate the portholes and ceilings, while orange, yellow and red sponges encrust the walls, making for terrific photo opportunities. Large schools of lemon butterflyfish and bluestripe snapper swarm approaching divers, while huge porcupine pufferfish hover just above the wreck. Keep your eyes peeled for the resident school of eagle rays and the rare Hawaiian stingrays that cruise the sandy surrounding area.

Toward the stern you can usually find several yellowmargin morays. Some have been fed by divemasters and tend to be quite friendly, but be respectful: don't touch them.

2 THE MAHI

Location: *Southwest of Waianae Boat Harbor*
Depth Range: *60-95ft (18-29m)*
Access: *Boat*
Expertise Rating: *Intermediate*

Once a fully intact wreck, the *Mahi* has recently begun to deteriorate. The wheelhouse and most of the upper decks have now collapsed to a point where you can no longer enter the wreck safely. However, this is truly still a terrific dive with lots to see and explore. Originally built for the US Navy, the 165ft-long ship was later converted into an oceanographic research vessel. Purposely sunk in 1982 as an artificial reef, the wreck has since become one of Oahu's most popular and exciting dives.

Diver with schooling banner butterflyfish found on the Mahi

3 KEWALO PIPES

Location: *West of Honolulu*
Depth Range: *40ft (12m)*
Access: *Boat*
Expertise Rating: *Novice*

This may not be the most dramatic site in Oahu, but it is a convenient, shallow dive that can be very enjoyable if you know what to look for.

The underwater steel pipeline is now broken into pieces, making an artificial reef that offers shelter to a variety of fish species. Near the pipe, look for devil scorpionfish, leaf fish and the endemic titan scorpionfish. These venomous (but slow moving) creatures are great photo subjects.

Surrounding the pipe at a depth of 30ft to 40ft you will find a coral reef consisting of several small ridges. A great variety of juvenile fish can be found within the protection of the finger coral, along with Potter's angelfish and some of the less common and endemic wrasses. The beautiful pearl wrasse, belted wrasse and shortnose wrasse are among the more intriguing endemic species.

In the rubble patches between reef structures you may encounter the small dragon wrasse, which resembles a piece of seaweed dancing over the rocks in the surge, or you might see the reptilian bottom-dwelling lizardfish. This is also an excellent site for spotting some of the Hawaiian islands' most colorful nudibranchs and octopuses.

4 MAGIC ISLAND

Location: *West of Honolulu*
Depth Range: *30-50ft (9-15m)*
Access: *Shore*
Expertise Rating: *Novice*

Known as Magic Island or Rainbow Reef, this site's popularity is mostly due to its location near Ala Moana Beach Park (north of Waikiki), along with easy shore access to the inside of the cove. Divers and snorkelers need to be aware of possible boat traffic in this area.

The first 100 yards from shore are shallow and offer only limited visibility, but the abundance of 'tame' hand-fed fish makes up for it. Here you'll be able to get quite close to a variety of fish that are normally skittish and hard to approach.

Other attractions for experienced fish-watchers are the juveniles and rare species found in this area. The sheltered lagoon makes an ideal home for many fish not normally found on open reefs. The area is also excellent for finding unusual and colorful nudibranchs.

Once you get out of the cove, the depth drops to about 50ft and water clarity improves. The terrain consists mostly of sand and coral formations with some cave formations in the channels connecting the cove with open water. With some luck you may encounter manta rays or sea turtles on this dive.

Fried egg nudibranch feeding on hydroids

Diver emerges from one of the coral encrusted pipes at Kewalo Pipes

Diver exploring YO-257 wreck

5 YO-257

Location: *West of Waikiki*
Depth Range: *55-100ft (17-30m)*
Access: *Boat*
Expertise Rating: *Intermediate*

This is a unique dive site in many ways. The former navy oiler was purposely sunk by Atlantis Submarine International, Inc. to serve as an artificial reef and attraction for their submarine-tour passengers. The 110ft-long vessel has rested upright in near-perfect condition on the sandy seafloor just off the shore of Waikiki since 1989.

During your dive you are likely to see an Atlantis submarine gliding by with all the passengers waving at you and taking snapshots from their dry environment. This is quite an unusual encounter and makes for an interesting dive. Be

Wreck Diving

Wreck diving can be safe and fascinating. Penetration of shipwrecks, however, is a skilled specialty and should not be attempted without proper training. Wrecks are often unstable; they can be silty, deep and disorienting. Use an experienced guide to view wrecks and the amazing coral communities that develop on them.

careful not to approach the submarine too closely, since its thrusters generate quite a bit of turbulence.

Although the submarine experience is fun, there is much more to see. The wreck's position on the sandy bottom makes it a veritable oasis in an underwater desert. Huge schools of friendly lemon butterflyfish, goatfish and bluestripe snapper swim around this marine-life magnet. The variety of nudibranchs near the sponges and hydroids is among the best you'll find anywhere in Hawaii. Expect to see green sea turtles, yellowmargin and whitemouth morays, porcupine pufferfish, boxfish, broomtail filefish and much more. If you're an inquisitive diver with a keen eye, you may find one of the well-camouflaged giant frogfish that live on the wreck.

Wide-angle photographers will be pleased by a variety of great photo opportunities, including images of *YO-257's* portholes, which are beautifully decorated with snowflake-like hydroids. Some portholes are accessible from the interior. If you plan to photograph your buddy peeking through one, warn them ahead of time that the hydroids have a nasty sting.

6 THE SEA TIGER WRECK

Location: *West of Waikiki*
Depth Range: *80-130ft (24-40m)*
Access: *Boat*
Expertise Rating: *Advanced*

Definitely one of Oahu's favorite wrecks, the *Sea Tiger* is more than 150ft long with several swim-throughs and penetration possibilities. Sunk in 1996 by a submarine company, the *Sea Tiger* doesn't have a lot of coral growth but does support a large number of schooling fish, moray eels, and nudibranchs. It is also common to see eagle rays circling the wreck.

The *Sea Tiger* rests upright on a sandy bottom at 130ft, but dive depth is generally between 80ft and 100ft. Apart from missing wood planks and some decay inside the wreck it is very much intact. Popular swim-throughs include the cargo holds mid-ship and the bridge, which allow for easy entry and exit. This is Hawaii's best wreck for penetration but nitrogen narcosis, together with a lot of silt, debris and loose wires,

makes it dangerous without the right training and experience. It's big enough to get lost in!

Snorkeler with green sea turtle

Throughout the world there are eight species of sea turtles. Green sea turtles are the most common species seen in Hawaii's tropical waters. They can grow up to 4ft (1.2m) long and weigh up to 300lbs (135kg). Hawksbill turtles – which reach up to 3ft (1m) in length and weigh as much as 165lbs (74kg) – also inhabit the region, though they are seldom seen by divers on reefs. Both species are endangered and protected by law: do not touch or molest sea turtles in any way.

Dangers contributing to the demise of these creatures include: hunting for human consumption, turtle-shell jewelry and ornaments; loss of habitat due to tourism and development; pollution; getting trapped in fishing nets; and injury from ship propellers and boat traffic.

What can you do to help turtles survive?

- don't disturb or frighten a sea turtle, especially during mating season (June through August)
- don't eat turtle eggs, turtle soup or any other turtle dish
- don't buy or use any product made from turtle shell
- encourage efforts to preserve turtle-nesting beaches as natural reserves.

Pyramid butterflyfish

7 BABY BARGE

Location: *Southwest of Diamond Head*
Depth Range: *45-85ft (14-25m)*
Access: *Boat*
Expertise Rating: *Intermediate*

The Baby Barge is not an impressive wreck in itself – it's fairly small and doesn't offer much in penetration or swim-through possibilities – but the surrounding reef is great. There is a cavern on the deep side of the wreck and it is not unusual to find one or two white tip reef sharks sleeping in it. Turtles are usually everywhere and seeing five or more is not uncommon.

The wreck lies at about 70ft, but if you want to check out the cavern the maximum depth will be 85ft. This is a good location for finding frogfish, Hawaiian lionfish, eels and several species of nudibranchs.

8 CORSAIR

Location: *Southwest of Diamond Head*
Depth Range: *107ft (32m)*
Access: *Boat*
Expertise Rating: *Advanced*

The Corsair is the only wreck visited by divers in Oahu that was not intentionally sunk as an artificial reef. While on a training mission off the coast of Hawaii Kai in 1946, the pilot ran out of fuel and safely bailed out before the plane plunged into the water southeast of Diamond Head.

Left to rest on the sandy bottom, the plane has become an oasis in an otherwise barren, current-swept seascape. Now embellished by colorful sponges and several coral structures, it shelters an interesting selection of fish species. Eagle rays and green sea turtles are among the larger residents which frequent the wreck. Due to the depth and the amount of things to see, this is a good site for nitrox-certified divers to extend their bottom time.

Hanauma Bay provides some of the best snorkeling in the islands

SOUTH COAST / HANAUMA BAY

Along the south coast, which extends from Diamond Head to Makapuu Point, you will find a panoramic coastline characterized by sheer cliffs and often pounding surf. This area also feels the grip of a treacherous current known as the 'Molokai Express,' produced by the prevailing northeast trade winds. This water movement is weakest near shore, so stay close when diving here.

Hanauma Bay, Hawaii's most scenic snorkeling spot (if you don't mind the crowds), is located along this coast. The bay, a marine life conservation district since 1967, attracts up to 10,000 visitors each day.

Part of the cone of this former volcano has collapsed into the ocean, forming a picture-perfect sandy cove protected from the elements. The water is calm almost every day of the year, making it perfect for first-time snorkelers.

Though Hanauma Bay has several sites that are interesting and appropriate for divers, not all sites are safely accessible from shore. Be sure to assess the weather, surf conditions and your physical ability before starting out.

9 TURTLE CANYON

Location: *Maunalua Bay*
Depth Range: *30-40ft (9-12m)*
Access: *Boat*
Expertise Rating: *Novice*

Turtle Canyon, just off the island's south coast, is the best place to spot green sea turtles on Oahu. You are almost guaranteed to see at least a few as you descend to the shallow reef, which has an average depth of only about 30ft. The turtles are most likely to be found resting on the rubble-covered sandy bottom or on the coral reef itself. Since they are accustomed to divers, they will usually allow you to get close, but please do not touch them!

This is a prime location to photograph these protected marine reptiles. A camera system with a 20mm or 28mm lens is ideal, but since the dive is so shallow and the light conditions are good, you can get decent shots even with a disposable underwater camera.

In addition to the resident turtle population, expect to see large schools

Divers exploring the Outside Reef

of durgeonfish (which tend to swarm divers), along with soldierfish and hermit crabs, shrimp, nudibranchs and other little creatures that live underneath the numerous overhangs and ledges. Be sure not to ignore the rubble patches, as they are home to interesting small animals as well.

Slate pencil sea urchins on lobe coral

10 INSIDE REEF

Location: *Hanauma Bay*
Depth Range: *5-20ft (2-6m)*
Access: *Shore*
Expertise Rating: *Novice*

As the most protected and shallowest area of Hanauma Bay, this site is more suitable for snorkeling than diving. Due to large crowds, the coral is no longer in good shape, and thousands of snorkelers and swimmers kick up sand, clouding up the water as the day progresses. The practice of feeding the fish with bread also contributes to poor visibility. For clearer and less-crowded conditions, it is best to dive or snorkel here is as early as possible: the park opens at 6am.

This is a perfect area for underwater photographers seeking to get good, close-up fish shots. The wide variety of butterflyfish are so tame that will swim right up to your lens, and the shallow depth allows divers to stay underwater longer.

Both adult and juvenile Picasso and lagoon triggerfish can be seen here. Rainbow-hued parrotfish are common,

along with an array of butterflyfish such as the endemic bluestripe butterflyfish, raccoon butterflyfish and largest of all, the stunning lined butterflyfish. Underwater photographers will be pleased to find that fast-swimming, shallow-water wrasses such as surge, Christmas and fivestripe wrasses – which all boast brilliant color patterns – are relatively easy to approach.

11 OUTSIDE REEF

Location: *Hanauma Bay*
Depth Range: *15-70ft (5-21m)*
Access: *Shore*
Expertise Rating: *Intermediate*

For more experienced snorkelers and divers, Outside Reef can be very rewarding. Visibility tends to be much better than at **Inside Reef**, the coral is in better shape and marine life is plentiful. As long as you don't go too far out, you'll still be within the protection of the bay.

The mostly sandy bottom and scattered coral heads at this site are inhabited by bluestripe, raccoon and threadfin butterflyfish, arc-eye hawkfish, Christmas and surge wrasses, triggerfish and tangs.

Caged shark diving has come to Oahu. At the time of writing there was one company offering this experience out of Haleiwa on the north shore.

Anyone can do this encounter with no certification required, there is also no age limit. The shark tour grounds lie about 3 miles offshore and takes about 15 minutes to get there from the harbour.

For more information on these tours see www.hawaiisharkencounters.com.

Schooling damsels and tangs are often found in the surge zone at Witch's Brew

To leave the inner reef and reach Outside Reef, do not attempt to swim over the barrier reef. This can be extremely hazardous, since any amount of surge can wash you across the surface of the coral. A passage known as 'the slot' provides a convenient entry and exit point between the inner and outer reefs. The slot is located on the right (southwest) side of the bay, in front of the lifeguard stand. A large cable runs through the channel near the surface, making a convenient guide back to the inner reef.

12 WITCH'S BREW

Location: *Hanauma Bay*
Depth Range: *40-50ft (12-15m)*
Access: *Shore*
Expertise Rating: *Advanced*

This is a particularly nice spot on the right (southwest) side of Hanauma Bay, found where a small peninsula juts out from shore. In front of this peninsula is a coral garden with a healthy marine life population.

The area got its name from the seething cauldron of multiple wave and current patterns that merge here, and form the area's wicked surge. Although the often-turbulent waters are the reason for the abundant marine life, they can make for a challenging dive.

One way to get to the site is to walk along the right-hand side of the bay until you reach the small peninsula. However, this is a long walk when carrying heavy scuba equipment, particularly if you are lugging underwater camera equipment as well.

The other option is to follow 'the slot' in Hanuama Bay through the barrier reef, then stay to the right and swim toward the peninsula.

Either way, Witch's Brew requires some 'commuting,' but it is worth it for more experienced and adventurous divers.

Building the Perfect Reef

The best way for divers to understand reef evolution is to observe artificial reefs at different stages of development. Artificial reefs can be made of any foreign object that has been submerged: ship or plane wrecks, 'junk' like tires, bottles and concrete blocks. Even broken-up wrecks with their component parts scattered about lend themselves well to marine life encrustation and are generally worth at least a couple of dives. The more you look, the more you'll see.

The abundance of marine life and coral growth on an artificial reef depends on three main factors:

Location: Reefs (both natural and artificial) provide animals with shelter from the current and predators. Artificial reefs placed in open, sandy areas become an oasis for surrounding marine life. This type of reef therefore tends to feature a denser concentration of marine life than on an open coral reef, where there are many more places to find shelter. The *Mahi* and the *YO-257* wrecks, both purposely sunk in large sandy areas, are good examples of this principle.

The shelter artificial reefs provide in current-swept locations often attracts species otherwise rarely seen. Juveniles also commonly take refuge while hydroids and sponges draw an abundant nudibranch population.

Material: Steel generally provides an easy surface for coral to grow on. Rubber and aluminum objects, though they may provide excellent shelter, are less suitable for coral growth.

Age: Coral generally takes at least a few years to establish itself. Other species are gradually attracted as the coral becomes more profuse. The longer an object has been underwater, the more populated and interesting the resulting artificial reef becomes.

WINDWARD SIDE

The shoreline between Makapuu Point and Kahuku Point on Oahu's windward side is only diveable during kona weather – for those few days when the trade winds are absent – which can occur occasionally throughout the year, but is more likely between November and April.

Slipper lobsters are common at Manana Island

13 MANANA ISLAND

Location: *Waimanalo Bay*
Depth Range: *40-70ft (12-21m)*
Access: *Boat*
Expertise Rating: *Advanced*

Manana Island is a seabird sanctuary just offshore from Sealife Park. Although this island appears to be close to shore, it is actually quite a distance and you should not attempt to dive this site without a boat.

Divers need to be aware that this site is frequented by the torrential Molokai Express current and should plan their dive accordingly. Be sure to follow your guide's instructions. The Molokai Express tends to bring clear water to this site, along with many large game fish such as trevally, tuna, billfish and sharks, including tiger sharks.

The best diving is found on the seaward side of the island and along a ridge that connects to adjacent Kaohikaipu Island. There are many overhangs along the ridge that are laden with lobsters and other crustaceans. Triton's trumpet shells, many species of beautiful cowries and other shelled snails are also commonly spotted along this ridge.

14 MOKU MANU

Location: *North of Mokapu Point*
Depth Range: *30-90ft (9-27m)*
Access: *Boat*
Expertise Rating: *Advanced*

Moku Manu is a two-island remnant of the Koolau Volcano.

Due to its location on the windward side of Oahu, this site is not dived frequently, so the rich environment and abundant marine life are pristine. Large

parrotfish, unicorn fish, tuna and trevally are common here.

There are several dive sites around the two rocky islands, but wind is generally the determining factor when choosing where to go. Also be aware of the strong, swift current that often sweeps between the islands and Mokapu Point: carefully assess the safety conditions of sites in this area before diving.

One of the most popular dive areas is a large cave between the two islands. The interior of the cave is dark, so be sure to bring a light to see the lobsters, crimson squirrelfish and soldierfish that inhabit the area. Outside the cave, you will encounter lush coral growth and an abundance of tropical fish. Green sea turtles are also occasionally spotted at the nearby sandy channel.

The seaward side of the northern island features a skirting shelf at 30ft that first drops to 90ft, then plummets below recreational diving limits. Along the shelf are numerous lava tubes and caves that are home to huge lobsters, yellowmargin morays and whitemouth morays. Tuna and other large fish are seen along the drop-off – just be sure to look toward the blue water to see what may swim by.

Lemon butterflyfish

Diver observing butterflyfish on steep drop-off

NORTH SHORE

Oahu's north shore, between Kahuku Point and Kaena Point, exhibits a ribbon of sandy beaches and numerous coves and bays. During winter months huge swells make this region undiveable, but during summer there are many good dive sites suitable for all levels.

Trumpetfish are commonly seen lurking under ledges

15 SHARK'S COVE

Location: *North of Waimea Bay*
Depth Range: *15-50ft (5-15m)*
Access: *Shore*
Expertise Rating: *Novice*

Named after a rock formation that loosely resembles a shark (an imaginative diver must have come up with the name), this site is one of the most popular along Oahu's north shore. During summer, when conditions tend to be calm, it is an excellent dive for novice divers and snorkelers, due to the lack of current and wave action. Shark's Cove also makes an ideal site for dive training, and instructors often conduct classes here.

Advanced divers are generally intrigued by the extensive tunnel and

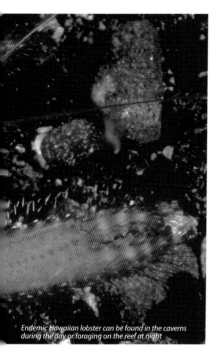
Endemic Hawaiian lobster can be found in the caverns during the day or foraging on the reef at night

16 THREE TABLES

Location: *North of Waimea Bay*
Depth Range: *15-50ft (5-15m)*
Access: *Shore*
Expertise Rating: *Intermediate*

Less than one mile down the road from **Shark's Cove** is an outstanding shore dive for intermediate and advanced divers. Named after the three flat off-shore lava rocks that break the surface of the water and then drop to 50ft, this site provides divers with spectacular seascapes including arches, overhangs, tunnels and small caverns. The best diving is found to the right, reached by swimming diagonally in the direction of **Shark's Cove**. Anticipate seeing a colorful medley of reef fish, lots of moray eels and even large conger eels.

If you swim farther out into deeper water you will also find a nice hard-coral reef inhabited by butterflyfish, Moorish idols and other colorful tropicals. Since Three Tables is located on the surf-prone north shore, you can safely access this site only during the summer months.

cave system found just outside the cove to the right. There is a lot to see at this site and the caverns are fun to explore, but be sure not to go beyond your level of training and comfort. If you are not familiar with the hazards of cave diving, it is recommended you enter only if accompanied by a professional dive guide.

With any surge present, cavern exploration can be disorienting and potentially hazardous. Even under calm conditions, sand and silt kicked up from divers' fins will cloud the water, making it easy to become disoriented.

This is also an excellent night dive, but unless you are an experienced diver and already familiar with the site and the local weather conditions, you should not attempt night diving without a guide.

During winter months this site is inaccessible due to high surf conditions.

Conger eel with cleaner shrimp

Hawaii The Big Island

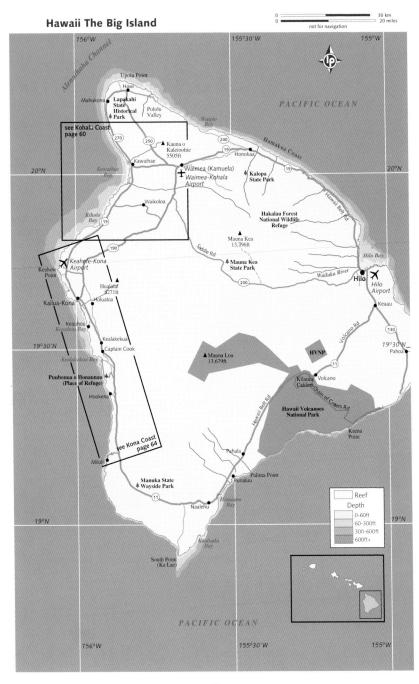

0 ————— 30 km
0 ————— 20 miles
not for navigation

Alenuihaha Channel

Upolu Point

Hawi

Mahukona

Lapakahi
State
Historical
Park

Pololu
Valley

Waipio
Bay

156°W

PACIFIC OCEAN

155°30'W

155°W

see Kohala Coast
page 60

270

250

▲ Kauna o
Kaleioohie
5505ft

240

Hamakoa Coast

Kawaihae

19

Honokaa

19

20°N

Kawaihae
Bay

✝ Waimea (Kamuela)
✈ Waimea-Kohala
Airport

Kalopa
State Park

20°N

Waikoloa

19

Hawaii Belt Rd

Kiholo
Bay

190

Hakalau Forest
National Wildlife
Refuge

▲ Mauna Kea
13,796ft

Saddle Rd

Hilo Bay

✈ Keahole-Kona
Airport

Keahole
Point

Hualalai
8271ft

▲

Holualoa

▲ Mauna Kea
State Park

200

Wailuku River

Hilo ✈
Hilo
Airport

Kailua-Kona

Keahou
Keauhou Bay

Kealakekua

Keaau

Captain Cook

Kealakekua Bay

Puuhonua o Honaunau
(Place of Refuge) ▲

▲ Mauna Loa
13,679ft

HVNP

Volcano Rd

19°30'N

130

Pahoa

Hookena

19°30'N

Kilauea
Caldera

Volcano

see Kona Coast
page 64

Hawaii Belt Rd

Hawaii Volcanoes
National Park

Chain of Craters Rd

Miloli

Kuena
Point

Manuka State
Wayside Park ▲

Pahala

11

Punaluu

Paliuu Point

Naalehu

Homuapo
Bay

Reef

Depth

0-60ft

60-300ft

300-600ft

600ft+

19°N

19°N

Kaalualu
Bay

South Point
(Ka Lae)

PACIFIC OCEAN

156°W

155°30'W

155°W

Big Island Dive Sites

Aerial view of the northern Kona Coast

The main island of Hawaii is known as the Big Island, and rightly so. As the largest tropical island in the Pacific, the Big Island has more land mass than the rest of the Hawaiian Islands combined. Its prominent high volcanos are often snow-capped in winter months and help provide a large leeward coast on the western side of the island. It is on this leeward side of the island along the sheltered, west-facing Kohala and Kona Coasts that you will find consistently superb dive conditions all year round. The eastern side of the island is exposed to the tradewinds and tends to be quite rough on the surface and less diver friendly. If you plan to dive the eastern coast, it is highly recommended you hire a professional and knowledgeable guide. A few dive shops in Hilo cater mostly to locals and offer guided shore dives.

Bluefin trevelly are often seen hunting in shallow water

KOHALA COAST

The Kohala Coast lies along the north-west, leeward shore of the Big Island. It is more influenced by the trade winds than the Kona Coast to the south and as a result is not always suitable for diving. However, when conditions are favorable, a number of dive sites are available – many of them featuring beautiful hard-coral gardens or fascinating lava formations.

Kohala Coast

	GOOD SNORKELING	NOVICE	INTERMEDIATE	ADVANCED
17 FROG ROCK	•	•		
18 PUAKO	•		•	
19 PENTAGON	•	•		
20 LEDGES				•

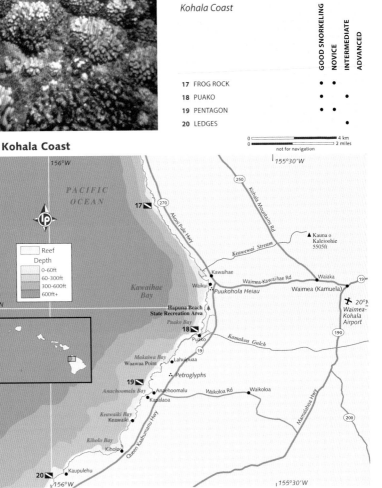

Kohala Coast

17 FROG ROCK

Location: *North Kawaihae Bay*
Depth Range: *20-60ft (6-18m)*
Access: *Boat*
Expertise Rating: *Novice*

Named after a rock on the shoreline that (with a little imagination) resembles a frog, this site is representative of north Kohala Coast diving. During your descent you'll find a lush and pristine hard-coral garden consisting mostly of finger and lobe corals.

Although reef fish are not as abundant here as they are along the Kona Coast, this tends to be a great area to see octopuses. It takes a keen eye to find one of these masters of camouflage. They are also masters of escape, and will elude you if you don't spot them before they spot you. Look at least 30ft in front of you to catch a glimpse of one before it has the chance to make a quick exit.

As you continue southeast along the coral reef you'll find several lava caverns and swim-throughs inhabited by sponge crabs, cowry shells and resident whitetip reef sharks. The rocks along the floors and walls of the caverns are beautifully encrusted with red and orange

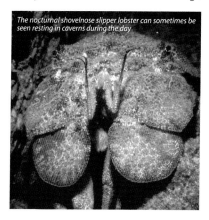

The nocturnal shovelnose slipper lobster can sometimes be seen resting in caverns during the day

sponges. Outside the caverns you'll find pufferfish, butterflyfish, filefish and other tropicals.

18 PUAKO

Location: *Puako Bay*
Depth Range: *30-90ft (9-27m)*
Access: *Shore*
Expertise Rating: *Intermediate*

This is an excellent dive in many respects. Several lava fingers extend from the rocky shore, each one featuring spectacular archways, swim-throughs, tunnels and countless crevices. This is a great site to look for crabs, Triton's trumpet shells, cowries, nudibranchs and much more.

If you follow the lava fingers from the shore you'll eventually reach the pristine finger-coral garden that is used as a resting area by about a dozen or more green sea turtles. Boat dives will most likely start in the coral garden and work their way up into the shallows along the finger reefs.

This dive can be performed as a shore dive, but only when the weather and water are extremely calm (though even this does not guarantee your safety). The afternoon winds are unpredictable and make diving here potentially hazardous. Waves that are suddenly kicked up by the wind can make shore entry and exit treacherous. Additionally, to reach the water you'll need to cross over sharp volcanic rock. Many local divers have a 'survival' story to tell about being caught in dangerous conditions while shore diving in this area, despite having entered the water while it was still glassy and calm. If you do decide to shore dive here, go early in the morning, when conditions are generally more stable. In any case, an experienced guide is highly recommended.

19 PENTAGON

Location: *Anaehoomalu Bay*
Depth Range: *20-30ft (6-9m)*
Access: *Boat*
Expertise Rating: *Novice*

When conditions are favorable, this shallow dive can be very enjoyable. Located just off the stunning beach at Anaehoomalu Bay, this site features a maze of interconnected tunnels, caverns and arches. The tunnel system has five large openings (hence the name), while numerous small openings and skylights allow sunlight to enter into this lava maze. You'll definitely benefit from using a flashlight to see the marine life that inhabits the tunnels. Crabs, shrimps, cowries and soldierfish are among the most common resident critters, but occasionally even Spanish dancers may be seen.

When water conditions are less favorable, surge can make tunnel exploration difficult or even hazardous and penetration is not recommended. The nice coral garden surrounding Pentagon makes it an interesting dive even if you don't enter the tunnels.

20 LEDGES

Location: *West of Kaupulehu*
Depth Range: *20-130ft (6-39m)*
Access: *Boat*
Expertise Rating: *Intermediate*

This terrific dive is located on the Kahuwai Reef, just off the beach by the Four Seasons and Kona Village resorts. There are two large ledges: one starts at 20ft and reaches 45ft, and the other starts at 60ft and drops below 160ft. Although it is possible to explore both ledges on one dive, divemasters often split the site into two to accommodate both novice and advanced divers.

Both ledges are characterized by sheer walls with countless overhangs and archways that are filled with crustaceans, shells and nocturnal fish such as soldierfish and squirrelfish. Whitetip reef sharks are frequently seen underneath the overhangs. Manta rays and spinner dolphins are often encountered near the shallower ledge, while the deeper ledge is home to large schools of pyramid butterflyfish, endemic bandit angelfish and even an occasional 300lb Hawaiian grouper.

Reticulated cowries are commonly found in the caverns and under ledges

KONA COAST

The Kona Coast stretches from Kea-hole Point to Kakio Point along the Big Island's western shore. Due to the island's massive mountains, this area experiences a sheltered lee that stretches several miles seaward and makes this one of the most desirable diving areas on the island. Calm water tends to be the norm, though during the winter months (when water conditions are more conducive to surfing) divers occasionally experience turbid water and limited visibility. About a mile offshore there is a steep drop-off where deepwater pelagics are commonly seen. The Kona Coast also boasts some of the Big Island's most pristine reefs and an abundance of exciting lava caves.

Kohala Coast

	GOOD SNORKELING	NOVICE	INTERMEDIATE	ADVANCED
21 GARDEN EELS/ MANTA NIGHTDRIVE	•	•		
22 PINETREES		•	•	•
23 TURTLE PINNACLE	•	•		
24 KAIWI POINT		•	•	•
25 MILEMARKER 4		•		•
26 KAHALUU	•	•		
27 MANTA RAY VILLAGE	•	•		
28 SHARKEY'S COVE		•		•
29 LONG LAVA TUBE		•		•
30 DRIFTWOODS		•		•
31 KEALAKEKUA BAY	•	•		
32 PLACE OF REFUGE	•	•		
33 ROB'S REEF	•			•
34 THREE ROOM CAVE				•
35 TUBASTREA TUNNEL				•

Snorkeling in Kealakekua Bay

Kona Coast

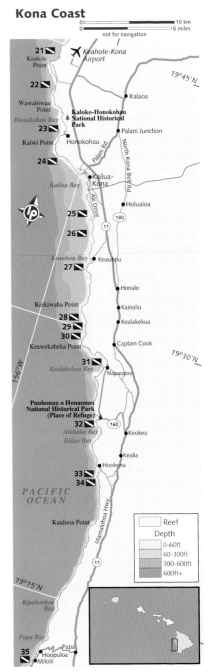

Spanish dancers can be found here on night dives

21 GARDEN EELS / MANTA NIGHT DIVE

Location: *North of Keahole Point*
Depth Range: *20-80ft (6-54m)*
Access: *Boat*
Expertise Rating: *Novice*

Most of the Kona operators come to do their manta ray night dive at this popular site, which has four moorings. In 2000 the Kona Surf Hotel in Keauhou Bay closed its doors and when the lights were turned off, the original Manta Ray night dive was no more. However, soon after the Kona Surf Hotel closed, it was discovered that a number of mantas frequented a northern bay near Keahole

point. Dive boats began to bring their own powerful lights, and along with the divers' lights, the mantas began to feed on the plankton the light attracted.

The dive site itself is a sloping reef that descends into a sandy bottom and a garden with eels by the hundreds.

As you move south, the coral on the sloping reef is quite pristine since it is protected from any southern swells. Divers will encounter a number of reef fish in this coral area, including the flame angel, parrotfish, raccoon butterflyfish and a large number of wrasses.

Since the reef slopes off quickly and the surrounding water is quite deep, it is also possible to encounter a variety of pelagics, including the manta rays, and even an occasional whale shark during a day dive.

Lizardfish are ambush predators that can be seen along the bottom laying in wait of their prey

22 PINETREES

Location: *South of Keahole Point*
Depth Range: *15-100ft (5-30m)*
Access: *Boat*
Expertise Rating: *Novice/Intermediate*

Pinetrees is a large area on the north tip of the Kona Coast that has more than eight excellent dive sites in close proximity. Many of these sites can be combined on a single dive and used to be clustered under one name, Pinetrees. Due to the installation of day-use moorings, each mooring now has a separate dive site name though they often are only a few yards away from each other. Pinetrees was originally named for the mangrove trees that used to be along the shoreline and were often misidentified. Popular sites in this area are Golden Arches, Pyramid Pinnacle, Skunk Hollow and Suck-um Up Cave, just to name a few. In these sites, divers will find several areas with fascinating lava formations, plus an abundance of diverse marine life.

This is one of the most popular dive areas for dive operators based in Kailua-Kona or Honokohau Harbor due to the quality of dive sites and close proximity of their base. Though the reef is often pounded by the surf in the winter – creating less-than-pristine dive conditions in and around the lava formations – divers will still encounter a wide variety of marine life away from the shoreline and shallow water. When calm enough, the lava tubes and archways near the shoreline support interesting reef life, as do the seaward rubble patches. Divers can encounter a large variety of moray eels including zebra, yellowmargin, dragon and whitemouth morays, as well as huge conger eels.

This is also a great spot to observe or photograph large schools of friendly butterflyfish and bluestripe snapper. One of the most popular critters here is the frogfish, which can grow to more than a foot long. These odd-looking creatures mesmerize novice and advanced divers alike.

23 | TURTLE PINNACLE

Location: *Honokohau Harbor*
Depth Range: *20-60ft (6-18m)*
Access: *Boat*
Expertise Rating: *Novice*

24 | KAIWI POINT

Location: *Pawai Bay, south of Kaiwi Point*
Depth Range: *15-130ft (5-39m)*
Access: *Boat*
Expertise Rating: *Novice/Intermediate*

This is the best spot along the Kona Coast to encounter turtles. Divers will often find them resting on the rubble-covered bottom and on the finger coral near the lava ledge. Often they can be observed at a cleaning station, where yellow tangs, convict tangs and goldring surgeonfish provide their services. Swarms of these little fish pick algae and parasites off the turtles' shells, keeping them clean, healthy and streamlined while reaping the benefits of an easy meal. The turtles are accustomed to divers and completely ignore their presence, which provides many terrific opportunities to photograph these friendly marine reptiles.

The fish life in this area is replete with schooling oval chromis and butterflyfish. As you swim toward shore, the terrain transitions into large boulders, where small frogfish and octopuses make their home. The shallows are also an excellent place to look for parrotfish, Christmas wrasses and surge wrasses.

Pawai Bay is the starting point for the Kaiwi Point dive and an excellent spot for novice divers and snorkelers due to protection from currents and shallow depth. The friendly fish are accustomed to being fed. In fact, the multitudes of lemon butterflyfish and black durgeonfish will rush to the surface to greet you.

The bottom of the bay is covered with finger coral, rubble patches and large boulders – perfect terrain for octopuses, wrasses and parrotfish. When conditions are calm, divers can explore the small caverns, nooks and crannies along the shoreline. The cavern ceilings are encrusted with tubastrea coral. At nighttime, when the polyps open up to feed, these corals resemble beautiful flower beds. As long as conditions are calm and you stay inside the bay, this site is an excellent night dive with plenty of swimming crabs, 7-11 crabs and reef lobsters crawling out of their daytime hiding spots.

More experienced divers will find the best diving toward Kaiwi Point, the dive site's namesake. The bottom slopes quickly down beyond 100ft, so be sure to watch your depth. You are likely to experience a current at the point, which in turn attracts abundant marine life. If you drop down the slope a bit, you may spot unusual fish species such as flame wrasses or longfin anthias. There have been quite a few whale shark and humpback whale sightings over the years, and manta rays, eagle rays and dolphins frequent the area.

Diver hovering above antler coral

Rockmover wrasses are commonly seen while snorkeling

25 MILEMARKER 4

Location: *South of Kailua-Kona*
Depth Range: *10-60ft (3-18m)*
Access: *Shore*
Expertise Rating: *Intermediate*

This dive site is popular with local divers. It is convenient and easy to find – just pull up to the side of Alii Drive at mile-marker 4. When conditions are calm, it's an easy and enjoyable dive. To enter the water you have to walk through a shallow area littered with lava rocks, so when the surf is up it is best to skip this dive.

The shallow cove is also a good snorkeling spot, without the crowds of nearby **Kahaluu**. The best diving is to the south, in deeper water near the exit of the cove. Here, you'll find a variety of shallow canyons with nooks, crannies and overhangs. There is also a small lava chimney that can be carefully entered on calm days.

This area also makes an exceptional night dive, with an array of crustaceans that emerge from the crevices to feed.

26 KAHALUU

Location: *South of Kailua-Kona*
Depth Range: *0-20ft (0-6m)*
Access: *Shore*
Expertise Rating: *Novice (inside bay only)*

Although diving is possible in Kahaluu, the bay is so shallow that most people simply go snorkeling.

This great spot is easily accessed by snorkelers and offers some of the best fish-watching opportunities on the Big Island.

To enter the water, follow the narrow natural channel that starts just below the lifeguard tower and winds its way through the lava rocks. Do not attempt to walk over the slippery and sharp lava rocks.

Once in the water, you are likely to encounter one of the resident sea turtles. Throughout the bay you'll find some of Hawaii's most colorful fish, including the humuhumu nukunuku apua'a (Picasso triggerfish), Christmas wrasses, butterflyfish and parrotfish.

On calm days you can dive outside the breakwater but be cautious of the offshore current. It has been known to sweep divers down the coast, necessitating a rescue mission by the Coast Guard.

27 MANTA RAY VILLAGE

Location: *Keauhou Bay*
Depth Range: *20-40ft (6-12m)*
Access: *Boat*
Expertise Rating: *Novice*

The original Manta Ray Village is located in front of the Sheraton Keauhou Bay Resort, formerly the Kona Surf Resort which closed in 2000. The Sheraton has reopened the resort and now does a Manta Ray education program nightly. Every night the hotel shines powerful lights on the water, which attracts plankton, and in, turn manta rays. Guests can observe the mantas nightly from the *lanai* (balcony) of their rooms or from special viewing areas within the resort's grounds. Each Monday, Wednesday and Friday from 7:45pm to 8:30pm James

L Wing, Kona Operations Manager for the Manta Network (a global organization for the protection and conservation of manta rays), and his interns answer questions and share information on manta behaviour and habitat.

Divers have seen up to 10 mantas at one time 'performing' their spectacular underwater show, but it is more common to find only a couple at a time. Although there is no guarantee that mantas will show up on any given night, dives during the new moon seem to be the best bets for manta encounters.

Since several dive operators have anchored here every night for years, the bottom terrain is not particularly good, but nocturnal marine life is surprisingly abundant. Spanish dancers, sleeping parrotfish, sleeping goatfish and beautiful cowries can all be found here, but all of these are generally outperformed by the mantas.

Snorkeling with the mantas can also be a fun and rewarding experience, but be aware that Manta Ray Village is in the middle of a boat channel. It is not recommended to dive or snorkel this site from shore, not only because of possible boat traffic, but also because the entrance over the sharp lava rocks can be extremely dangerous. Snorkel charters to Manta Ray Village are run from Keauhou Bay.

Several mantas are commonly seen at night at both Big Island manta ray dive sites

Tiger cowries are nocturnal but can be found in the daytime just within the caverns and under overhangs

28 SHARKEY'S COVE

Location: *South of Keikiwaha Point*
Depth Range: *25-50ft (8-15m)*
Access: *Boat*
Expertise Rating: *Intermediate*

Named after a whitetip shark that used to be seen dozing underneath one of the overhangs, this site is near Red Hill, an area distinguished by a red cinder cone that has been partly eroded by the sea. Above the red cinder, a large patch of green catches one's eye, hence the dive site is also known as Meadows.

Along the shoreline you can explore several large lava tunnels, caverns and a beautiful archway, all of which provide opportunities for some nice wide-angle photographs.

A variety of crustaceans, including swimming crabs, slipper lobsters and sponge crabs, are frequently spotted inside the lava formations. Underneath the overhangs you'll find Hawaiian tur-

The potter's angelfish is usually found darting among the finger coral

keyfish, multicolored nudibranchs and beautiful tiger cowries. Occasionally, barracuda can be observed cruising the shallows. The healthy finger reef that extends perpendicularly to the coastline is home to an abundance of reef fish. You'll find largemouth lizardfish, devil scorpionfish and octopuses residing in the areas of rubble and sand that surround the reef.

This site offers one of the best night dives on the Kona Coast. After dark, the reef is literally crawling with Spanish dancers, slipper lobsters, spiny lobsters, moray eels and partridge tun shells.

29 LONG LAVA TUBE

Location: *South of Keikiwaha Point*
Depth Range: *15-60ft (5-18m)*
Access: *Boat*
Expertise Rating: *Intermediate*

Long Lava Tube is a little south of Sharkey's Cove (but still within the Red Hill area) and features one of the longest lava tubes in Hawaii. Several skylights allow light to penetrate through the ceiling, but overall the tube is dark enough that you may see active nocturnal species even during the day. Crabs and other crustaceans, morays and even Spanish dancers make the tube their residence. Be sure to bring your dive light to illuminate what Long Lava Tube has to offer.

Outside the tube you'll find countless other lava formations that shelter critters such as conger eels, Triton's trumpet shells and schooling squirrelfish.

Take a compass reading of the sheer-sided cinder-cone cove before you start your dive. To finish, swim toward this shore. You'll come across a couple of gorgeous reefs that feature an abundance of marine life, as well as a large patch of rare, soft leather coral.

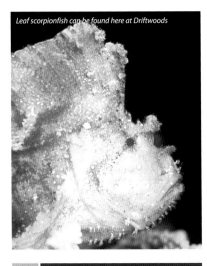
Leaf scorpionfish can be found here at Driftwoods

that occasionally sweep through this region. The uncommon bandit angelfish is often seen here below 70ft, along with psychedelic wrasses, bridled triggerfish and redspotted sandperches. In the shallower areas of the reef you are likely to see moray eels and perhaps even a spotted snake eel.

31 KEALAKEKUA BAY

Location: *Kealakekua Bay*
Depth Range: *10-130ft (3-39m)*
Access: *Boat*
Expertise Rating: *Novice (shallows only)*

30 DRIFTWOODS

Location: *North of Keawekaheka Point*
Depth Range: *15-80ft (5-24m)*
Access: *Boat*
Expertise Rating: *Intermediate*

This site is characterized by two lava fingers that run perpendicularly to the shore. The fingers start at a shallow plateau, where you'll find a series of caves, overhangs and lava formations that shelter Hawaiian pipefish, slipper lobsters, sponge crabs and other crustaceans.

The smaller of the two fingers, located to the south, starts in about 15ft of water and extends seaward until it ends abruptly with the top of the finger at 30ft and the bottom at 60ft. The other lava finger to the north provides the main attraction of the dive. It continuously drops as it extends seaward until it flattens out and blends into the finger-coral reef at 120ft.

Both lava fingers, particularly the deeper one, attract a great variety of marine life, probably due to the currents

This is where Captain Cook, the 'official discoverer' of the Hawaiian Islands, was killed in 1779. The spectacular backdrop of sheer lava cliffs and ancient Hawaiian burial sites makes this sheltered bay a fantastic place to visit. Below the surface it's just as beautiful. Pristine coral gardens that begin in the shallows at 15ft and continue down to 100ft make this a wonderful site for both snorkelers and divers.

The abundant marine life includes friendly fish as well as rare species and numerous moray eels. Experienced fish-watchers will recognize the beautiful flame angelfish, saddleback, raccoon and oval butterflyfish, blacktail snapper and other rarities. It's an excellent area to spot leaf fish, lizardfish, frogfish, turkeyfish and some of the biggest trumpetfish.

Kealakekua Bay is also home to a resident pod of dolphins, whose clicking sounds are commonly heard underwater in the winter months. Though it is rare to see a humpback whale while diving, divers can often hear them singing. Toward the point, encounters with manta rays and whale sharks are possible.

Diver videoing manta ray at night

The Manta Ray night dives present unique and consistently good opportunities to photograph these magnificent creatures. Once the mantas establish their feeding pattern, they tend to ignore divers. The best way to observe and photograph the mantas is to remain somewhat stationary and allow them to approach you. Encounters within a foot or so are common. Still, there are several things that make photographing the mantas at night a challenge. Your chances of getting a good shot are much better if you are prepared with the right equipment, and know how to use it to your advantage.

Photographers will find the greatest difficulty is the low-level light at night. If shooting digitally, you may want to consider increasing the sensitivity (ISO) to a faster speed. For film shooters, pushing your film a stop or two will compensate a little for the lack of ambient light (some films are designed to be pushed up to 1000 ASA). However, you must realize that you will need to adjust your settings to compensate not only for the mantas' very reflective underbelly, but also for their black top side, which absorbs the strobe flash. It is best to choose and then shoot several times from the same basic angle and distance while bracketing to increase your chances of capturing an image with the correct exposure.

Because the dark top side of the rays contrasts little with the dark aquatic background, most auto-focus systems will have trouble. One way around this is to focus on the white underside, where you are likely to find gill slits and sometimes black spots that provide enough contrast for most auto-focus cameras to function.

You may also have difficulty composing your shots with a camera that has a small viewfinder. It can be difficult to see the partially black rays in the surrounding darkness. Shooting a manual-focus housing with a large sports viewfinder, or a Nikonos camera with a 15mm or 20mm lens and the appropriate viewfinder, along with two strobes is recommended. Set the focus to the desired distance and shoot as soon as the manta is within your focal range or depth of field.

32 PLACE OF REFUGE

Location: *Puuhonua o Honaunau Bay*
Depth Range: *10-120ft (3-36m)*
Access: *Boat or Shore*
Expertise Rating: *Novice (shallows only)*

Also known as Puuhonua o Honaunau Bay, this area features Hawaii's best shore dive in regard to accessibility, coral growth and marine life. A natural lava step is used as an entrance point. Be sure the surf is down when you enter – and especially when you exit – otherwise this area can be hazardous.

Once you are in the water you'll be able to see a sandy patch to the right at 30ft where some energetic diver constructed a big ALOHA sign made out of bricks years ago. To the left of the entrance area you'll find several small canyons with overhangs and many nooks and crannies. These are good areas to see crabs, moray eels and sea turtles. If you swim straight out, the bottom drops quickly down to below 130ft. You'll find some of the most beautiful finger-coral and plate-coral formations along this drop-off.

Snorkeling is excellent in the shallow water along the edges of the bay, where you'll see pristine lobe-coral gardens and an abundance of surgeonfish and tangs, including inquisitive yellow tangs.

White spotted dolphins seen off the Kona Coast

33 ROB'S REEF

Location: *South of Hookena*
Depth Range: *30-100ft (9-30m)*
Access: *Boat*
Expertise Rating: *Intermediate*

Rob's Reef (also known as Twin Sisters) features a vast finger-coral garden home to a variety of fish that tend to be less common in other areas. Brilliant flame angelfish, flame wrasses, psychedelic wrasses and smalltail wrasses are just some of the beautiful residents.

Two lava ridges extend at right angles from the shore to about 50ft. Start your dive along the south ridge.

Blue-Water Diving

Blessed with very calm waters and a coastline that drops quickly to several fathoms, the Kona Coast offers the unique opportunity to see pelagic species in the open ocean while blue-water diving. A few miles offshore, adventurous divers may encounter whitespotted and bottle-nosed dolphins, pilot whales, pelagic sharks, marlin and other large game fish. However, taking the plunge into the clear, blue water is not for the fainthearted. Free diving and scuba diving in blue water can be extremely hazardous due to the potential of disorientation and should not be performed without proper safety measures and professional guidance. A reference line, drift line and proper surface support are but a few of the elements necessary to safely enjoy the blue-water experience. One must keep in mind that locating marine life miles offshore can be a challenging task, leaving the best chances of success to operators who offer blue-water adventures on a regular basis.

Diver observing whitespot damselfish in the antler coral at Rob's Reef

Once you have passed both ridges, return to the shoreline and you'll find yourself approaching a giant two-story cavern beautifully embellished with red, yellow and orange encrusting sponges.

Be sure to check out the coarse black sand surrounding the ridges for the unusual crocodile snake eel. These bizarre critters bury themselves in the sand, leaving only their heads exposed. Their color may range from blood-red to white.

34 THREE ROOM CAVE

Location: *South of Hookena*
Depth Range: *40-80ft (12-24m)*
Access: *Boat*
Expertise Rating: *Advanced*

This is one of the best cave dives along the Kona Coast. There are no skylights or windows, so expect the interior to be dark. Though the three large, two-storey-deep chambers invite divers to explore, this dive should only be made with the proper safety equipment – use a line for reference, have backup lights and backup tank with regulator.

In the farthest and darkest chamber, mole lobsters and candycane shrimp can sometimes be seen. Both are species that will never emerge into the open light.

The other chambers are inhabited by Hawaiian, spiny and bull's-eye lobsters, sponge crabs, cowries and many other photogenic critters. The outside of the cave is another dive in itself.

The abundance of interesting creatures makes this region special. Colorful harlequin shrimp can be found here, along with snake eels, hairy hermit crabs, octopuses and much more.

This is definitely a dive not to be missed, but do be aware of potentially strong currents.

35 TUBASTREA TUNNEL

Location: *West of Milolii*
Depth Range: *20-90ft (6-27m)*
Access: *Boat*
Expertise Rating: *Advanced*

Tubastrea Tunnel is situated about 600ft from shore right in front of the fishing village of Milolii, which has long benefited from the rich fishing grounds in this area. This is a spectacular dive site, but the currents can be raging, so don't attempt to approach this site from shore.

Underwater, at about 35ft, you'll find a huge lava tunnel that is entirely encrusted with tubastrea coral. The tunnel is open on both ends and short, though dimly lit, inside. A flashlight is useful to get a better look at the marine life, but is not needed to find your way from end to end.

Some frogfish can grow up to the size of a football

Near the tunnel, you are likely to find an incredible array of unusual cowries, nudibranchs and even frogfish. Although the tunnel is the main attraction, there are various other canyons, caverns and overhangs along the shoreline. The seafloor slopes from about 60ft to 90ft. Drop seaward down the slope and you'll likely spot a wide range of unusual critters. Dragon morays, colorful nudibranchs, snake eels, octopuses and tiger morays can all be added to this site's animal inventory.

Advanced divers will also appreciate Tubastrea Tunnel as a night dive, with the reef and tunnel walls literally crawling with interesting nocturnal critters.

Lava archways and caverns are found at Tubastrea Tunnels

Photographing Lava Formations

Hawaii's many lava caverns, archways, tunnels and tubes provide exciting photo opportunities. By utilizing a strobe light, you can take advantage of the colors of the encrusting sponges and tubastrea corals and bring out their rich red, bright orange and yellow hues to produce some dazzling images.

You can also work with the natural sunlight to produce silhouetted, wide-angle and scenic shots. Many of the caverns have solid shapes, skylights or windows that lend themselves to interesting compositions and provide good contrast. Placing the radiant sunbeams within the frame of your photograph will help to create drama, while a diver in the background will add depth to your image. Shoot at an upward angle and use a fast shutter speed of at least 1/250 to sharpen the shimmering sunbeams.

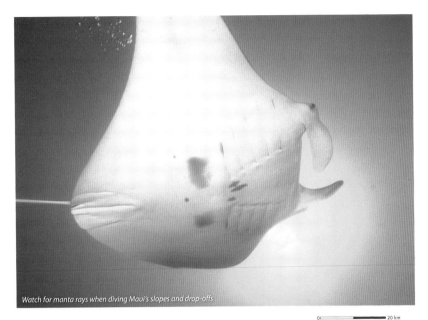
Watch for manta rays when diving Maui's slopes and drop-offs

Maui County Index

0 ⎯⎯⎯ 20 km
0 ⎯⎯⎯ 10 miles
not for navigation

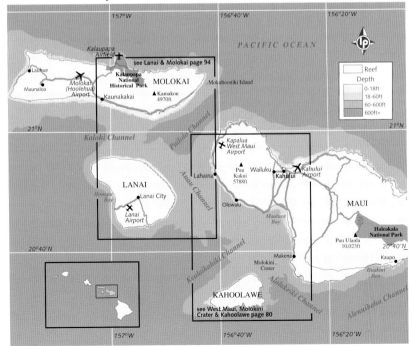

157°W   156°40'W   156°20'W

PACIFIC OCEAN

Kalaupapa Airfield

see Lanai & Molokai page 94

Kalaupapa National Historical Park

MOLOKAI

• Lauhue

Molokai (Hoolehua) Airport

• Maunaloa

▲ Kamakou 4970ft

• Kaunakakai

Mokuhooniki Island

Reef

Depth
0-18ft
18-60ft
60-600ft
600ft+

21°N   21°N

Kalohi Channel

Pailolo Channel

Kapalua West Maui Airport

LANAI

• Lanai City

✕ *Lanai Airport*

Honopu Bay

▲ Pau Kukui 5788ft

Lahaina •

• Wailuku

Kahului ✈ *Kahului Airport*

Olowalu •

Auau Channel

Maalaea Bay

MAUI

Haleakala National Park

▲ Puu Ulaula 10,023ft

• Kaupo

Hoikini Bay

20°40'N   20°40'N

Kealaikahiki Channel

• Makena

Molokini Crater

KAHOOLAWE

see West Maui, Molokini Crater & Kahoolawe page 80

Alalakeiki Channel

Alenuihaha Channel

157°W   156°40'W   156°20'W

78

Maui County Dive Sites

Maui County includes Maui, the tiny Molokini Crater, Kahoolawe, Lanai and Molokai.

Maui is renowned for luxurious resorts and fancy restaurants, but still has plenty of unspoiled places: a combination that makes the island popular with honeymooners. Molokini Crater, the tip of an extinct volcano, rests halfway between Maui and Kahoolawe. The uninhabited island of Kahoolawe once served as a religious center for native Hawaiians, but from 1939 to 1990 was used for live bombing and shelling, first by the US Army and then the US Navy. The island is now being restored to facilitate Hawaiian cultural and spiritual activities again. Lanai is a relatively unspoiled but small and barren island, once home to Dole's pineapple plantations. With production ceased, the island is now concentrating on attracting tourism. Molokai is still charmingly rural and slow paced and is only lightly visited by tourists.

These islands once formed a single large island, but the ocean eventually filled in the low-lying areas and separated the land into four individual land masses (with the tip of Molokini Crater still above water, too). The channels between these islands are exception- ally shallow, providing ideal breeding and nursing grounds for North Pacific humpback whales. Be on the lookout for these gentle giants during winter while above and below the water.

Diving Maui generally means the opportunity to dive its close neighbours, Lanai Molokini and Molokai. Because of this, Maui County is often said to have the most diverse diving in all the Hawaiian islands, with lava formations, vertical walls and calm sheltered bays.

Over the past few years the Maui diving community has begun a movement toward the creation of artificial reefs in sand areas largely devoid of life. The sinking of the 97ft *Carthaginian* on December 13, 2005 was the first phase of a project developed by Atlantis Submarines that involves placing additional vessels and/or engineered artificial reef structures to create new reefs in two separate drop zones. Each drop zone is planned to cover about a half-acre area approximately 3100ft off Puamana Beach Park, and be about 100ft deep. This is deep enough for divers to access but not too shallow to be a hazard to surface navigation. The creation of these wreck dives/artificial reefs makes Maui even more diverse.

Bird's-eye view of Maui's coastline

West Maui, Molokini, Crater & Kahoolawe

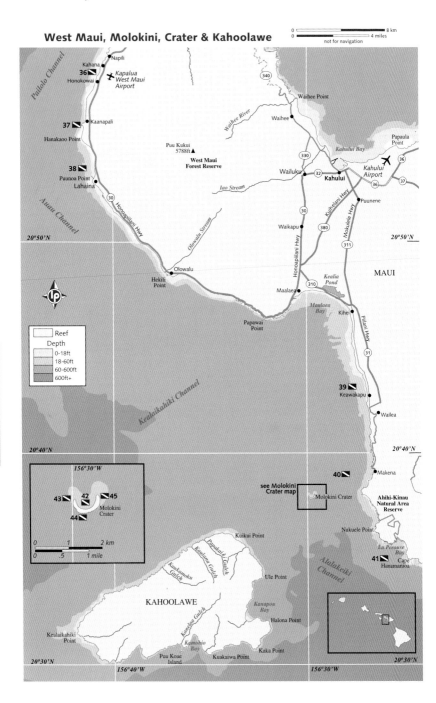

0   8 km
0   4 miles
not for navigation

Pailolo Channel

Napili
Kahana
Honokowai
36
Kapalua West Maui Airport

Kaanapali
37
Hanakaoo Point

Auau Channel

Puu Kukui
5788ft▲
West Maui Forest Reserve

38
Punnoa Point
Lahaina

Honoapiilani Hwy

Waihee Point

Waihee River

Waihee

Kahului Bay

Papaula Point

340

330

Puunene

Wailuku

Kahului

Kahului Airport

36

37

Iao Stream

32

380

Olowalu Stream

Waikapu

Waiapu

Mokulele Hwy

311

30

Honoapiilani Hwy

Kuihelani Hwy

20°50'N

20°50'N

MAUI

Olowalu

Hekili Point

Maalaea

310

Kealia Pond

Maalaea Bay

Kihei

Pilani Hwy

Papawai Point

Keauhakahiki Channel

39
Keawakapu

Wailea

31

20°40'N

20°40'N

Reef
Depth
0-18ft
18-60ft
60-600ft
600ft+

40

Makena

see Molokini Crater map

Molokini Crater

Ahihi-Kinau Natural Area Reserve

156°30'W

43   **42**   **45**
44
Molokini Crater

0   1   2 km
0   .5   1 mile

Kuikui Point

Kaukamoku Gulch

Papakaiki Gulch

Kaulana Gulch

Ule Point

Nukuele Point

La Perouse Bay

41
Cape Hanamanioa

Alalakeiki Channel

KAHOOLAWE

Kanapou Bay

Halona Point

Kealaikahiki Point

Kanloa Gulch

Kamohio Bay

Puu Koae Island

Kuakaiwa Point

Kaka Point

20°30'N

20°30'N

156°40'W

156°30'W

MAUI

The second largest Hawaiian island, Maui arose from the ocean floor as two separate volcanoes. Lava flows and erosion eventually built up a valley-like isthmus between the two, linking them in their present form. The southeastern portion is dominated by Haleakala, and the northwest by Puu Kukui. The two high peaks block the trade winds that blow in from the northeast.

Maui's best and most consistently good dive sites are found along the leeward shore that winds down from Kaanapali to **La Perouse Bay.** Although the north shore is Maui's longest coastline, this region is seldom dived due to its remoteness and year-round rough water. The windward southeast coast is also rarely visited because of near-constant winds, swells and strong currents.

West Maui, Molokini Crater & Kahoolawe

	GOOD SNORKELING	NOVICE	INTERMEDIATE	ADVANCED
36 BLACK ROCK	•	•		
37 HYATT REEF	•	•		
38 CARTHAGINIAN WRECK			•	
39 ST ANTHONY			•	
40 FIVE CAVES	•		•	
41 LA PEROUSE	•		•	
42 INSIDE CRATER	•	•		
43 REEF'S END			•	
44 BACK WALL				•
45 ENENUE			•	

36 BLACK ROCK

Location: *Southeast of Kahana*
Depth Range: *15-30ft (5-9m)*
Access: *Beach*
Expertise Rating: *Novice*

Black Rock is probably not the most thrilling shore dive on Maui, but it is the easiest, safest and most convenient. A large, black volcanic-rock peninsula juts out several hundred feet from the otherwise sandy shore in front of the Sheraton Hotel. The south side of the peninsula borders and protects the bay, which is a perfect playground for novice divers and snorkelers. The area is also a popular night dive suitable for all levels.

The underwater terrain consists mostly of sand and volcanic rock. Marine life highlights include a large variety of friendly fish. Expect to be approached by large swarms of butterflyfish and tangs. Used to being fed, their appearance provides good snapshot opportunities in shallow water.

More experienced divers may want to leave the cove, which is easiest to do near the reef along the peninsula. You'll be rewarded with better visibility and more natural marine life behavior, but be prepared for a moderate current once you reach the peninsula's point.

Ornate butterflyfish are commonly seen here at Black Rock

37   HYATT REEF

Location: *West of Kaanapali*
Depth Range: *40-50ft (12-15m)*
Access: *Boat*
Expertise Rating: *Novice*

This reef is not far offshore in front of the Hyatt Regency Hotel, but is too distant to be reached from the beach. The highlight here is the resident green sea turtle population so accustomed to divers that they tend to ignore them. You'll generally find the turtles resting on the rubble-covered bottom, on the finger coral, or on their way to the surface to breathe while they make great photo opportunities, but please don't ride, touch or harass these animals. Green sea turtles are protected and there are hefty fines for disturbing them in any way.

The dive site consists of several reef areas interspersed with patches of sand. You may find cone shells, helmet shells or little sand gobies.

As you drop deeper the coral transforms into a rubble area where octopuses are commonly seen. You may also see devil scorpionfish, rockmovers and spottail dartfish. As you learn to identify these critters, the apparently barren rubble suddenly becomes much more interesting.

This site also features several large antler-coral trees that often host the endemic whitespot damselfish. As you drop down the slope, watch out for potentially strong currents.

Cone shells may be found in the sandy areas at Hyatt Reef

38 CARTHAGINIAN WRECK

Location: ½ mile offshore between the Puamana and Launiupoko parks in Lahaina.
Depth Range: 65-95ft (20-28m)
Access: Boat
Expertise Rating: Intermediate

The *Carthaginian II* was built in 1920 as a commercial bulk carrier and sailed the Baltic Seas until it was converted into a replica of a whaling supply vessel in 1973. From then until its sinking in December 2005 it served as a floating 'whaling days' museum in Lahaina harbor. It now rests upright on its keel in 95ft of water with the mast starting in 65ft.

At the time of writing, the vessel had only just been sunk, so there was no growth on it, however the 97ft, steel-hulled vessel is expected to develop into a self-sustaining habitat for fish, coral and other marine life. It will also provide a new and interesting site for scuba divers, helping to alleviate over-use of natural reefs along the Lahaina coastline. The wreck's location will have no impact on swimming or surfing.

39 ST ANTHONY

Location: *Keawakapu Beach.*
Depth Range: *60ft (18m)*
Access: *Boat*
Expertise Rating: *Intermediate*

Just offshore from the Renaissance Wailea Beach Resort, this fishing trawler was sunk in 1997 to a depth of 60ft amidst an existing artificial reef. Along with the deposit of hundreds of concrete-weighted tires, in which marine

Carthaginian before she was intentionally sunk

animals have taken up residence, the area has become home to over 50 species of fish.

The wreck itself has been gutted to allow adventurous divers to enter the boat and explore the site from the inside out. Resident turtles have taken to lying on the deck while schools of goatfish circle and dart around divers. It is also common to see two resident frogfish on the deck, nicknamed 'The Captain' and 'Little Buddy.'

40 FIVE CAVES

Location: *West of Makena*
Depth Range: *40ft (12m)*
Access: *Boat or Shore*
Expertise Rating: *Intermediate*

This site is called Five Caves or Five Graves. Either way, you can't go wrong. It features several caves and caverns, and is located in front of a cemetery of five Japanese graves that marks the dive's entry point.

Although this site is frequently visited by dive boats, it is also a quality shore dive for experienced divers, though the entrance is a rocky one, so be cautious! Because this area has become popular for launching kayaks and small powerboats, it can sometimes get a little crowded.

From shore, swim through the natural channel to reach the dive site. After swimming past the wash rocks (the partially submerged rocks that get washed over when the surf is up), descend to the two lava fingers that run perpendicular to the shore. These lava formations are punctuated by a series of caverns, arches and overhangs filled with crimson Hawaiian bigeye fish, soldierfish and crustaceans.

Divers frequently report encounters with turtles, moray eels and conger eels, and occasionally even whitetip sharks.

Five Caves is also a popular night dive. If you are planning a night shore dive, you should be very familiar with night diving logistics. Avoid shore diving here at night, or whenever any wave action is present.

Whitesaddle goatfish can be observed foraging in the rubble areas

Deep Diving

Opportunities to dive deep abound in Hawaii. Many attractions are beyond 130ft (40m), the recognized maximum depth limit of sport diving. Before venturing beyond these limits, it is imperative divers are specially trained in deep diving and/or technical diving.

Classes will teach you to recognize symptoms of nitrogen narcosis and proper decompression procedures when doing deep or repetitive deep dives. Remember, emergency facilities in Hawaii are limited and can be difficult to reach. Know your limits and don't push your luck when it comes to depth.

41 LA PEROUSE

Location: *La Perouse Bay*
Depth Range: *10-60ft (3-18m)*
Access: *Boat or shore*
Expertise Rating: *Intermediate*

This site is found at the end of Makena Alanui Road in the middle of the scenic La Perouse Bay. The bay is a fairly recent creation in Maui's geological history, formed by a lava flow about 200 years ago.

A lava-rock pinnacle runs perpendicular to the shoreline, rising from the seafloor at 60ft to 10ft below the surface.

The Corsair wreck off Oahu is an example of a deep dive

Slate pencil sea urchins look menacing but are harmless to divers

Located approximately a quarter of a mile from shore, this pinnacle requires a bit of a swim and diving here can only be recommended when conditions are calm.

Most divers first notice the abundance of slate pencil urchins, one of the few urchin species not only pretty, but also harmless to divers.

The shallows also often harbor Triton's trumpet shells along with a variety of sea stars. The fish are very friendly here, and divers can even approach the timid bird wrasse.

You can explore several nice caverns inhabited by squirrelfish and bigeye fish. Check smaller crevices for crabs, ghost shrimp or banded coral shrimp.

Out in the open you are likely to see endemic bluestripe butterflyfish, banded angelfish, flame angelfish, schools of goatfish and perhaps even turtles.

La Perouse is one of the sites in Hawaii where you may also encounter a barracuda or two and, if you swim out to the site's most seaward point, you could get lucky and catch a glimpse of spinner dolphins cruising by.

Night diver with porcupine pufferfish

Hawaii boasts some of the best night diving in the world. After dark, the reefs come alive with an awesome diversity of crustaceans and other critters that are hidden in the lava caverns, nooks and crannies during the day. Many are brilliantly colored, such as the flame-orange Hawaiian and bull's-eye lobsters, the multicolored regal slipper lobster, the scarlet Spanish dancer and the Hawaiian swimming crab.

Night diving provides macro photographers with an excellent opportunity to get close to their subjects. Most reef fish are found in a dormant state in and around the coral, which allows you to closely observe and photograph many species that are skittish during the day. Many of the fish also take on different, more sombre color patterns at night.

There is no need to penetrate caves and lava tubes, since most nocturnal creatures will be roaming the open reef. Moray eels are commonly encountered hunting for their prey, while cowries can be observed in the open, utilizing their mantles as camouflage.

Those shooting with a Nikonos system will find a close-up kit or a 1- to 2-macro extension setup to be rewarding. When shooting a housed camera, a fixed 1-to-1 macro lens such as a 60mm or 105mm lens can also produce outstanding results. Be sure to rig a spotter flashlight onto your system so that you don't find yourself shorthanded. Aiming the light beam directly at the animal may cause it to retreat. Photographers generally fare best when the subject is lit by only the outer glow of the light.

MOLOKINI CRATER

The tip of this extinct volcanic crater rises out of the water in the channel between Maui and the uninhabited island of Kahoolawe.

While the northern side has been breached by the ocean, the southern half of the crater is still intact, creating a crescent-shaped island of volcanic rock barely a quarter of a mile (400m) long. The crater can be divided into four main diving areas: inside, outside, and the two points of the crescent.

Molokini is a designated marine life conservation district. All boats visiting must use the moorings rather than anchors in order to keep coral damage to a minimum, but the high volume of divers has certainly affected the reef over the years.

If you prefer to avoid the crowds, try to find an operator that visits in the afternoon.

Tour operators occasionally offer two morning dives on the outside of Molokini, then move to the inside after most other boats have left.

42 INSIDE CRATER

Location: *Molokini Crater*
Depth Range: *10-30ft (3-9m)*
Access: *Boat*
Expertise Rating: *Novice*

This is by far Maui County's most popular spot for snorkeling, snuba and scuba diving. The inside of the crater is almost always protected from the wind and current, is accessible year-round and is suitable for all levels of divers and snorkelers.

The bottom's mix of rubble and sand with scattered rock and reef formations provides an ideal habitat for a variety of species. There are zillions of butterflyfish, saddle wrasses, chubs, surgeonfish, parrotfish and bluestripe snapper, all of which fearlessly approach divers and snorkelers. Octopuses, moray eels, leaf fish and other friendly critters can also be found within the crater's sheltered cove.

Humpback Whale Tales

Humpback whales belong to the filter-feeding baleen whale family. Instead of bony teeth they have baleen – rigid strips made of a material similar to human fingernails – that they use to filter small fish, krill and other crustaceans out of the water.

North Pacific humpback whales migrate from their summer feeding grounds near Alaska and British Columbia to winter in the Hawaiian Islands, where they reproduce, calve and nurse from October to May.

Divers most often see humpbacks at the surface spraying water from their blowholes, or as they partake in playful tail and fin slapping. Occasionally divers are lucky enough to observe a full breach, when a whale propels up to two-thirds of its body out of the water. Whales are sometimes seen underwater, though they are more likely to be heard 'singing'. Whale songs are unique compositions of squeals and groans that can cover a great distance.

Humpback whales are endangered mammals and are protected throughout the Hawaiian National Marine Sanctuary. They may not be approached within 300ft (90m) by boats, divers or snorkelers.

Bluestripe snappers are common throughout the Hawaiian Islands

43 | REEF'S END

Location: *Molokini Crater*
Depth Range: 60-100ft (18-30m)
Access: *Boat*
Expertise Rating: *Intermediate*

Reef's End is an excellent site for more experienced divers. This dive usually starts on the inside edge of the northern, submerged part of the crater. Establish your neutral buoyancy then work your way around the point toward the outside of the crater, where visibility is generally much better than inside.

The topography consists of huge lava slabs and large boulders beautifully encrusted with red sponges. This site also features massive antler coral swirling with damselfish.

You'll find many mated pairs of butterflyfish, including the less common oval (also called redfin) butterflyfish and

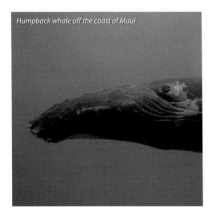
Humpback whale off the coast of Maui

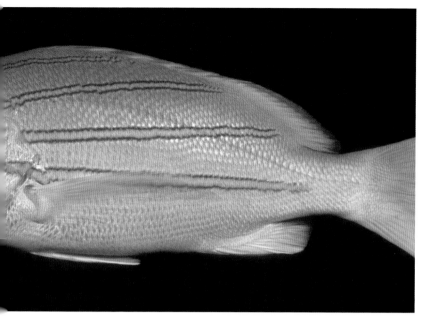

saddleback butterflyfish. As you come around the point, keep your eyes open for whitetip reef sharks.

This is also a good site to encounter a variety of eels. Many are accustomed to divers and will poke their heads out of their holes when divers are near. Though some can be closely approached, be aware that not all eels are diver-friendly. Keep a healthy respect for these wild animals to ensure a safe dive.

44 BACK WALL

Location: *Molokini Crater*
Depth Range: *Surface-130ft (39m)*
Access: *Boat*
Expertise Rating: *Advanced*

The Back Wall (also called the Outside Wall) of the crater is a spectacular experience and rates as one of the best dives in Hawaii. The dramatic black, sheer

crater wall with its colorful sponges, schooling fish and often crystal-clear water is simply breathtaking.

Due to the makeup of the site and drift diving logistics, the Back Wall is only suitable for fairly experienced divers. Since the wall drops vertically from the surface to beyond recreational depth limits, perfect buoyancy control is a necessity.

Covered with red and orange encrusting sponges, the wall boasts several black-coral trees, wire corals and endless nooks and crannies that often contain critters such as cowries, shrimps, nudibranchs and even long-handed lobsters.

Particularly noticeable are colorful fish that naturally form large schools, unlike the solitary fish in other popular locations that look for handouts from divers. You are likely to see large swirls of pennant, raccoon and pyramid butterflyfish. Reef sharks and larger pelagic fish such as wahoos and tunas are also common.

Mantas are often seen on the current-sweet point of Enenue

45 ENENUE

Location: *Molokini Crater*
Depth Range: *50-130ft (15-39m)*
Access: *Boat*
Expertise Rating: *Intermediate*

Enenue is the Hawaiian name for rudderfish. This site is named for its abundance of these silver-gray members of the sea chub family, which are generally looking for a handout when they rush to greet you.

Although the beginning of this dive is pretty easy, it becomes more challenging as you follow the southern inside crater wall toward the point. The base of the crater wall levels off to a wide shelf. Here you should look for octopuses, moray eels and the unusual snake eel. If you have keen eyes, you may even spot a rare boarfish.

The shelf eventually plummets deeper than 130ft. If you continue along the wall toward the often current-swept point, you have a good chance of seeing big fish such as tuna, mantas, and wahoo. There have also been whale shark sightings reported in this area.

When diving off of an anchored boat, it's usually best to turn around once the point is reached, but the dive can also be performed as a drift dive. In this case, you continue around the point and dive along the crater's back wall until your gauges indicate it's time to come up.

KAHOOLAWE

This is now closed to the public and was never a popular dive area, due to it having been used as a bombing range.

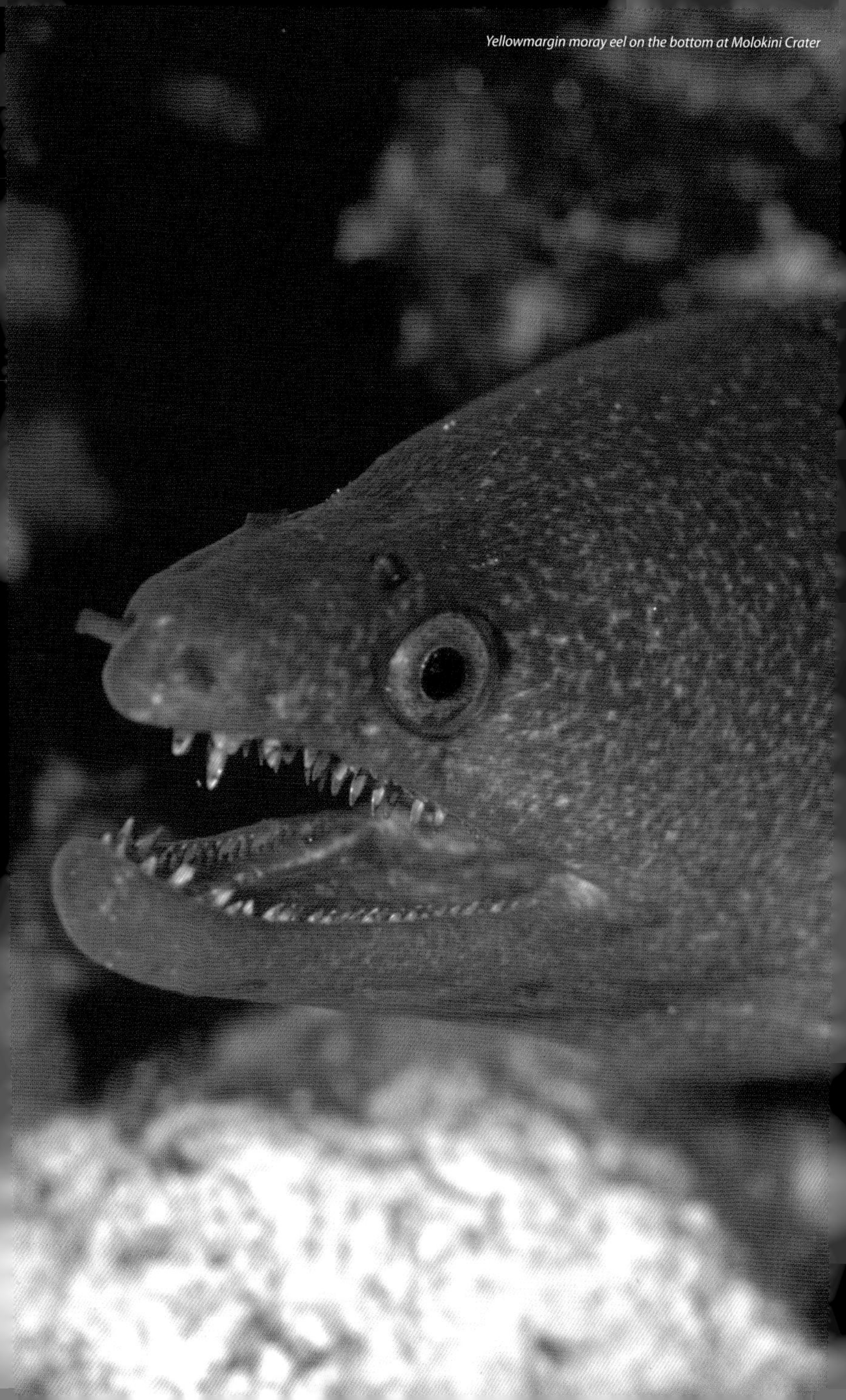

Yellowmargin moray eel on the bottom at Molokini Crater

Lanai & Molokai

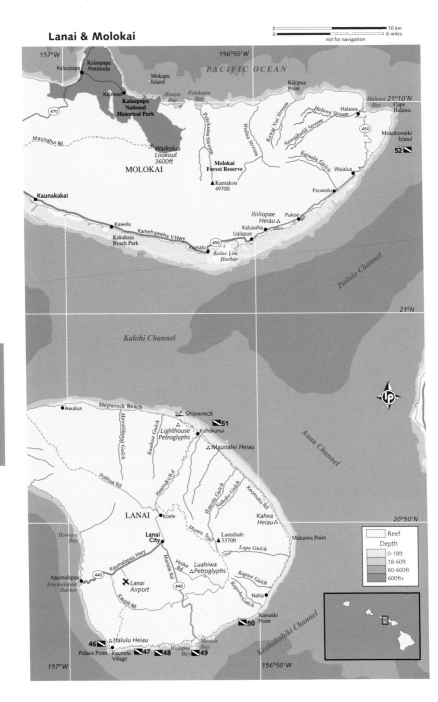

0 ━━━━━━━━━ 10 km
0 ━━━━━━━━━ 6 miles
not for navigation

157°W   156°50'W

PACIFIC OCEAN

Kalaupapa
Kalaupapa
Peninsula
Kalaupapa
Mokapu
Island
Kikipua
Point
470
Kalawao
Kalaupapa
National
Historical Park
Haupu
Bay
Pelekunu
Bay
21°10'N
Halawa
Bay
Cape
Halawa
Maunahui Rd
Waikolu
Lookout
3600ft
Pelekunu Stream
Wailau Stream
Halawa Stream
Kawela Nui Stream
Nawaihulili Stream
Halawa
450
Mokuhooniki
Island
52

MOLOKAI
Molokai
Forest Reserve
Kainalu Gulch
Kaunakakai
▲Kamakou
4970ft
Waialua

Kawela
Kamehameha V Hwy
Iliiliopae
Heiau
Pukoo
Pauwalu
Kakahaia
Beach Park
450
Kamalo
Kaluaaha
Ualapue
Kalae Loa
Harbor
Pailolo Channel

21°N

Kalohi Channel

Awalua
Shipwreck Beach
Shipwreck
51
Kahokunui
Lighthouse
Petroglyphs
Maunalei Heiau
Auau Channel

Hauolilino Gulch
Kaohua Gulch
Keomuku Rd
Polihua Rd
Hanalo Gulch
Nahaka Gulch
Keomuku Rd

LANAI
Koele
Munro Trail
Kahea
Heiau
20°50'N
Lanaihale
▲3370ft
Makaiwa Point
Lanai
City
Honopu
Bay
Kaumalapau Hwy
440
Manele Rd
Hoike
Rd
Luahiwa
Petroglyphs
Lopa Gulch
Kapua Gulch

Kaumalapau
Kaumalapau
Harbor
440
× Lanai
Airport
Kaupili Rd
Naha
Kaapahu Gulch

Reef
Depth
0-18ft
18-60ft
60-600ft
600ft+

Kamaiki
Point
50

46
Halulu Heiau
Palaoa Point
Kaunolu
Village
47
48
Hulopoe
Bay
49
Manele
Bay
Kealaikahiki Channel

157°W   156°50'W

Orange cup corals and red encrusting sponge can be found on the current side of the rock at Shark Fin

LANAI

Lanai lies 9 miles (14km) south of Molokai and 9 miles west of Maui. Lanai means 'hump' in Hawaiian; when viewed from Maui, the island resembles the back of a whale rising out of the water. Dramatic cliffs and barren landscape are distinct characteristics of Lanai. Though formerly used for ranching and plantations, it is increasingly the domain of luxury resorts.

Divers will find amazing underwater caves, caverns and tunnels along Lanai's south coast, which offers the best and most protected diving on the island.

Lanai & Molokai	GOOD SNORKELING	NOVICE	INTERMEDIATE	ADVANCED
46 SHARK FIN	•	•		
47 WASH ROCK	•	•		
48 PYRAMIDS			•	
49 FIRST & SECOND CATHEDRALS			•	
50 SERGEANT MAJOR & SERGEANT MINOR		•		
51 TURTLE HAVEN			•	
52 FISH RAIN				•

46 SHARK FIN

Location: *Northwest of Palaoa Point*
Depth Range: *20-90ft (6-27m)*
Access: *Boat*
Expertise Rating: *Novice*

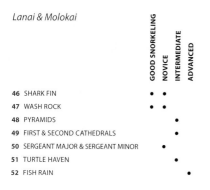

A lava formation resembling a shark's dorsal fin marks this site. The underwater terrain consists mostly of lava rock, with a lava finger running perpendicularly from shore.

Generally, the dive starts at the fin-shaped rock, then slowly travels along its submarine extension, which is characterized by jagged lava concealing a great amount of marine life within its nooks and crannies.

Due to frequent currents flowing through this area, one side of the rock is beautifully embellished with orange cup coral and vast blankets of red encrusting sponges. It is also an excellent spot to locate moray eels and octopuses.

Although coral growth is sparse, this site is popular with snorkelers due to the large school of lemon butterflyfish that rush to the surface to greet them.

If you are an accomplished free-diver, it's fun to dive down along the fin rock to see the same colorful scenery that divers enjoy.

47 WASH ROCK

Location: *South Lanai*
Depth Range: *Surface-60ft (18m)*
Access: *Boat*
Expertise Rating: *Novice*

Wash Rock is a great dive with lots of variety and color. This large lava pinnacle barely protrudes above the surface and its tip is often awash in the breaking swells. It is perhaps due to this constant water movement that the upper part of the pinnacle is blanketed with a variety of colorful sponges. A small school of bluestripe snapper are often found dashing in and out of the overhangs. With the varied color and ample light

you will find many excellent photo opportunities.

A short swim will bring you to the 'tunnel of love', a lava tube where you are likely to find a mated pair of yellowmargin moray eels. The area outside the tunnel is great to poke around in, with interesting critters to be found. Inquisitive divers may even spot an elusive octopus.

Octopus swimming

Safe Diving in Lava Caves

Many of Hawaii's top dive sites center on the region's unique and exciting lava formations, created when molten lava flowed into the ocean. The outer layer of the lava flow cooled and solidified when it came into contact with the water, creating hollow tubes, tunnels, archways and a multitude of caves and caverns. These fascinating formations (now home to an array of marine life) are usually a diver's dream, but can quickly turn into a nightmare if safety concerns are ignored.

Strong surge, loss of light, disorientation and complicated interconnecting tunnel systems can be serious hazards. A diver should only consider cave penetration when accompanied by an experienced guide familiar with the cavern. Consult your dive guide on any special safety equipment that may be needed and, of course, whether conditions are safe to dive.

When entering an overhead environment, divers should adjust buoyancy to be slightly negative to reduce the effect of any sudden surge movement. Always move slowly and keep plenty of space between you and the diver in front in order to avoid having your mask kicked off or your regulator pulled out of your mouth by their fins. The less finning, the better; if you must kick, simple foot-ankle movements are best. Remember, if you don't feel comfortable entering overhead environments, there is nothing wrong with staying behind, preferably with a dive buddy, and enjoying the outside of the cave.

Lanai is world famous for it's underwater lava formations

48 PYRAMIDS

Location: *South Lanai*
Depth Range: *40-120ft (12-37m)*
Access: *Boat*
Expertise Rating: *Intermediate*

Pyramids, with lava arches and pinnacles, to expanses of finger corals and reef fish, is a diver's playground. Named for the great number of schooling pyramid butterflyfish commonly found at the top of the pinnacles, the site offers some of Lanai's best diving.

From the mooring, a short swim south takes you to a large, hollow lava pinnacle. The numerous nooks and crannies in its sides shelter a high concentration of marine life. Schools of bluestripe snapper swim near the soft snowflake and black corals, while lobster and cleaner shrimp hide behind the thick swarms of nocturnal squirrelfish that part in the beam of dive lights. Several eels make their home here as well, including sizable yellowmargin moray eels and the vicious-looking viper moray. Shy pipefish also hide in small cracks and, with a little luck, you may be able to view a sleeping whitetip reef shark.

Leaving the pinnacle, lava arches are found about 120ft to the west. These swim-throughs are laced with pretty snowflake coral. Lobsters, crabs and large cowry shells can often be found in the archways. Throughout the dive site, solitary barracuda may also be spotted.

Sand channels another 40yd west offer helmet shells, peacock flounder

Hawaiian spiny lobster with swirling nocturnal squirrelfish

and the sand-diving razor wrasse. Only recently discovered as a dive site, Pyramids is quickly becoming a favorite.

49 FIRST & SECOND CATHEDRALS

Location: *Southeast of Hulopoe Bay*
Depth Range: *20-65ft (6-20m)*
Access: *Boat*
Expertise Rating: *Intermediate*

First and Second Cathedrals, Lanai's most famous and certainly most spectacular dive sites, are located along the island's south shore. First Cathedral is about 3 miles east of Second Cathedral. These sites feature huge, two-storey-high underwater grottoes.

Both grotto systems consist of arches, tunnels, ridges and passageways that are sensational to explore. Inside you'll find rich marine life that includes lobsters, crabs, cowries and bright-red soldierfish.

First Cathedral can be entered through a tunnel leading into a huge chamber that provides divers with a fantastic light show. When the sun is out, light streams into the chamber through the porous lava ceiling. The laser-like rays dance through the interior, reminiscent of a cathedral's stained glass windows.

Enter the Second Cathedral through a wide crack in a wall. There are two main chambers whose ceilings are blanketed with tubastrea coral; a black-coral tree hangs down from the ceiling of one chamber. Light also enters here through side cracks, but it is not as dramatic a show as in First Cathedral.

Though the grottoes are accessible most of the year, be especially cautious in the shallow areas that have ceiling holes if there is any surge present. Water funneling through can force you through the water or slam you into the sharp lava formations.

Schooling bluestripe snappers

50 SERGEANT MAJOR & SERGEANT MINOR

Location: *Southwest of Kamaiki Point*
Depth Range: *25-50ft (8-15m)*
Access: *Boat*
Expertise Rating: *Novice*

Sergeant Major is a great dive site for divers who like to poke around, look into every hole and peek under every ledge. There is a ton of marine life on this dive, as well as interesting topographic formations. Three ridges run seaward, two of which are connected by a beautiful archway. Whitetip reef sharks are occasionally seen near the archway or the ridges along with the usual tropical fish and turtles found in the region.

A large sandy area separates Sergeant Major from its counterpart, Sergeant Minor. The latter's claim to fame is a 50ft-long lava tube with a huge (but friendly) moray eel slinking around inside. If you get the chance to take a close look at the eel, be sure to check for cleaner shrimp that may be present on or around its face. These shrimp are known for their bravery and ability to clean a multitude of teeth in a very short period of time.

Both Sergeant Major and Sergeant Minor face the open ocean, so be sure to turn your eyes to the deeper water at least occasionally – large game fish, dolphins and (from October through May) humpback whales may be seen cruising the area.

51 TURTLE HAVEN

Location: *Northeastern Lani*
Depth Range: *20-65ft (8-20m)*
Access: *Boat*
Expertise Rating: *Intermediate*

Located on the northeast corner of Lanai is one of the best stretches of hard coral reef found in Maui County.

Exposure to the prevailing trade winds makes Turtle Haven a rarely accessible site to dive.

However, when the winds do calm down, this site offers a virtual coral garden inhabited by a variety of reef fish, including several species of parrotfish, wrasses and butterflyfish.

Within this pristine garden it is common to see a gathering of turtles that appear to be socializing while having their shells cleaned at the cleaning station.

Sergeant major fish

Diver photographing yellowtail coris

Humpback whales can sometimes be seen diving Fish Rain

MOLOKAI

This rural, slow-paced island offers little tourist hype to accompany its deserted beaches, spectacular valleys and historical sites. All of Molokai's dive sites are located around the small offshore island Mokuhooniki. Due to lack of protection from wind and waves, dive sites are accessible only on perfectly calm days, which are rare. The area is subject to very strong currents and dives are usually performed as drift dives. Only advanced divers should sign up to go diving at Molokai.

52   FISH RAIN

Location: *Mokuhooniki Island*
Depth Range: *80-130ft (24-39m)*
Access: *Boat*
Expertise Rating: *Advanced*

Fish Rain is perhaps Molokai's most exhilarating dive, with dense schools of fish constantly cruising overhead. You are likely to see more fish here than on most other dives in Hawaii.

Kalaupapa

On Molokai's central north shore lies the Kalaupapa Peninsula, surrounded on three sides by some of Hawaii's roughest waters and on the fourth side by the world's highest sea cliffs.

It was here that lepers were sent into exile to prevent the spread of leprosy, which was introduced to the Hawaiian islands during the 19th century. Father Damien, a Catholic missionary, arrived at Kalaupapa in 1873. He erected more than 300 dwellings, installed a water system and nursed the sick until succumbing to the disease himself in 1889.

Since the 1940s, sulfone antibiotics have controlled leprosy (now called Hansen's disease) successfully, and all of the fewer than 100 patients are free to leave. But Kalaupapa Peninsula is the only home this older population knows and most choose to stay. Today, tourists may visit the peninsula, but they are required to take a guided tour to minimize their impact on this community.

Another big attraction is the possible sighting of 'serious' pelagic animals. Hammerhead sharks, tiger sharks, whale sharks, humpback whales and monk seals have all been seen at this site at one time or another.

The site itself is along the outer slope of an underwater cinder cone that rises from 150ft to the surface of the water. It can only be accessed when weather and water conditions permit the boat-crossing from Maui.

Even when the crossing can be made, currents may be very strong on this dive.

Hawaiian swimming crab

Diver peering into lava tube

Kauai & Niihau

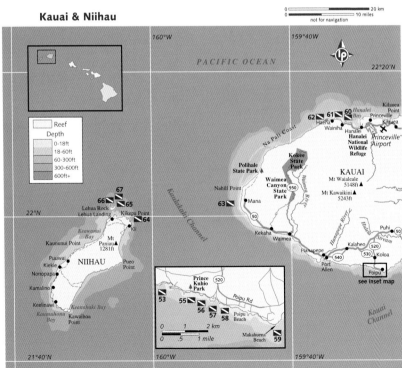

0 ⌐⎯⎯⎯⎯⎯⎯⎯ 20 km
0 ⌐⎯⎯⎯⎯⎯⎯⎯ 10 miles
not for navigation

PACIFIC OCEAN

160°W

159°40W

22°20'N

Na Pali Coast

Hanalei Bay

62 ◣ 61 ◣ 60 ◣

Haena

Wainiha

Kilauea Point

Princeville

Kilauea

Hanalei

Hanalei National Wildlife Refuge

Princeville Airport

Polihale State Park

Kokee State Park

Waimea Canyon State Park

KAUAI

Mt Waialeale 5148ft ▲

Mt Kawaikini 5243ft ▲

Nahili Point

Mana

63 ◣

550

Hanapepe River

Waimea River

Puhi

50

Kekaha

Waimea

Kalaheo

520

Koloa

530

Hanapepe

540

Poipu

see inset map

Port Allen

Kauai Channel

67 ◣
66 ◣ ◣ 65

Lehua Rock
Lehua Landing

Kikepa Point

64 ◣

Kii

22°N

Kaununui Point

Keawanui Bay

Mt Paniau ▲ 1281ft

Pueo Point

Puuwai

Kiekie

NIIHAU

Nonopapa

Kamalino

Keelinawi

Kawaihoa Point

Keanahaki Bay

Kaumuhonu Bay

Kaulakahi Channel

Reef

Depth
- 0-18ft
- 18-60ft
- 60-300ft
- 300-600ft
- 600ft+

Prince Kuhio Park

520

Poipu Rd

53 ◣

55 ◣

56 ◣

57 ◣ 58 ◣

Poipu Beach

Makahuena Beach

59 ◣

0 ⌐⎯ 1 ⎯ 2 km
0 ⌐ .5 ⎯ 1 mile

21°40'N

160°W

159°40'W

Kauai & Niihau Dive Sites

Squirrelfish can be found schooling in caverns by day and foraging the reef at night

Covered by lush tropical forest, Kauai is aptly nicknamed the 'Garden Island.' With stunning scenery and scant development, it is a mecca for hikers, kayakers and other adventurers. Niihau, Kauai's closest neighbor, is generally referred to as the 'Forbidden Island.' This small, dry, windswept island has been privately owned since 1864 and limited numbers of non-Hawaiians are permitted to visit.

When weather conditions are favorable, Kauai and Niihau offer some unique and exciting dive opportunities. The islands' positions on the northern edge of the warm-water coral belt and the fact that their shorelines are prone to large swell impacts mean that corals are not as abundant as they are along the southern Hawaiian Islands. What the region lacks in coral reefs it makes up for with exciting lava formations, unusual fish species and pristine diving conditions.

KAUAI

Kauai is the fourth largest of the Hawaiian Islands, with an area of 558 sq miles (1445 sq km). If you are looking for lush scenery, this is the place to find it. The North Shore is green and mountainous with waterfalls, beautiful beaches and stream-fed valleys. The northwest coast is lined by the steeply fluted Na Pali sea cliffs, Hawaii's foremost hiking destination.

Though summer trade winds keep the heat down, Kauai's climate changes more with location than season and tends to be more varied than the other islands.

Excellent dive sites are found around the island but overall access is less reliable than around the rest of the Hawaiian Islands due to Kauai's less-predictable weather conditions. Sites located along the dramatic North Shore are undiveable during the winter months, and even the south shore spots can be sketchy at times. Although there are good novice dive spots on Kauai, some of the prime sites are better suited to more experienced divers.

Kauai Dive Sites

	GOOD SNORKELING	NOVICE	INTERMEDIATE	ADVANCED
53 GENERAL STORE			•	
54 TURTLE BLUFFS			•	
55 PK		•		
56 KOLOA LANDING		•		
57 AMBERS ARCHES			•	
58 SHERATON CAVERNS		•		
59 BRENNECKE'S LEDGES			•	
60 OCEANARIUM				•
61 TUNNELS REEF		•		
62 KEE LAGOON		•		
63 MANA CRACK				•

Turtles are common on many Kauai dive sites

53 GENERAL STORE

Location: *West of Kukuiula*
Depth Range: *50-80ft (15-24m)*
Access: *Boat*
Expertise Rating: *Intermediate*

Located on Kauai's south shore, General Store is so named because it is a site with something of interest for everyone. It is home to the remains of the steamship *Pele*, which sank on March 25, 1895 after running aground on Kalaniupao Rock about a quarter of a mile away. Unfortunately, Hurricane Iniki scattered the already battered pieces of the wreck in September of 1992, but you can still recognize the propeller, several anchors and some of the ground tackle.

The site is perhaps most noteworthy for its wide variety of marine life. Along the seaward side of a large u-shaped ledge are three sizable lava caves cradling rare critters such as brilliantly colored ghost shrimp and Hawaiian pipefish. Pipefish are small, elongated fish that – due to their cryptic habits and camouflaging abilities – are rarely seen, but once spotted tend to be quite approachable.

Along the wall, you'll find several black-coral trees home to longnose hawkfish, a popular macrophotographer's subject. You may also find large schools of the endemic lemon butterflyfish, bluestripe snapper, turtles and whitetip reef sharks.

of the rare morwong and whiskered boarfish adds to the attraction. Watch out for strong currents and rough surface conditions.

55 PK

Location: *West of Prince Kuhio Park*
Depth Range: *20 (6m)*
Access: *Shore*
Expertise Rating: *Novice*

Named after its location just offshore from Prince Kuhio Kalaniana'ole's birthplace near Poipu Beach, PK is an ideal site for novice divers and snorkelers. The shallow depth, lack of current and relative protection from wave action make the site well suited for divers' first open water dives. Interesting lava formations and abundance of marine life ensure that more-experienced divers also enjoy this site.

There are countless nooks and crannies where you may find pretty shells or colorful shrimp. Friendly reef fish are seen throughout the dive, including rainbow-hued parrotfish, brilliantly colored butterflyfish and elegant angelfish.

54 TURTLE BLUFFS

Location: *East of Poipu Beach*
Depth Range: *40-90ft (6-27m)*
Access: *Boat*
Expertise Rating: *Intermediate*

A small seamount at the center of this dive site serves as a cleaning station for turtles. The turtles appear to show a desire for socializing with one another, and there are usually quite a few relaxing together.

Underneath the ledges you'll sometimes find white-tip reef sharks dozing in the sand. Eagle rays and mantas are occasionally sighted, and the presence

Parrotfish sleeping in a mucus cocoon at night

56 KOLOA LANDING

Location: *East of Poipu Beach*
Depth Range: *5-55ft (2-17m)*
Access: *Shore*
Expertise Rating: *Novice*

Hawaiian lionfish are often seen in the lava tubes and hiding under ledges during the day

Undoubtably Kauai's favourite shore dive, Koloa Landing is also great for snorkeling. Before Hurricane Iniki raged through Kauai, the sandy bottom at this old boat landing featured anchors, old bottles and fittings from 18th- and 19th- century whaling ships and trading vessels, as well as a huge antler coral. Unfortunately, many of these have gone and only occasionally, after a storm can you spot some of the artifacts in the sand. But the horseshoe-shaped reef still makes an excellent dive site for beginners, featuring nice lobe coral, schooling blue-stripe snappers, moorish idols and some rare species, such as saddleback butterflyfish, flying gumards and dragon morays. It is also common to observe resident turtles and baby eagle rays here and the marine life overall is abundant.

57 AMBERS ARCHES

Location: *Poipu Beach*
Depth Range: *40-80ft (12-24m)*
Access: *Boat*
Expertise Rating: *Intermediate*

Ambers Arches is one of Kauai's premier dives and home to many unique fish and invertebrates. It offers some great topography which includes black coral trees decorated with as many as six Hawaiian lionfish at once. The great fish life at this site includes pipefish, wormfish, puffers, frogfish, anthias and more, and there's an abundance of invertebrates, such as sponge crabs, yellow hairy hermits mantis and ghost shrimp. Shark and turtle sightings are common. Be sure to explore the underside of the arch, the ceiling of which is carpeted in beautiful tubastrea coral.

58 SHERATON CAVERNS

Location: *Poipu Beach*
Depth Range: *35-65ft (11-20m)*
Access: *Boat*
Expertise Rating: *Novice*

Also known as The Circus, this dive has become one of Kauai's most popular sites for novice and advanced divers alike. It's conveniently located near Poipu Beach, enjoys relative protection from the swells and offers lots to see.

Three huge lava tubes run perpendicularly to the shoreline in front of the Sheraton Kauai Hotel in Poipu. Both the inside and outside of the tubes are an underwater photographer's heaven. Upon entering the tubes, look for spiny lobsters, reef crabs, 7-11 crabs and shrimp. You may even find a Spanish dancer or turkeyfish hiding inside.

Rare schooling bicolor anthias can be seen at Ambers Arches

Resting white-tip reef sharks are commonly found underneath the overhangs at Brennecke's Ledges

Be sure to take a good flashlight and don't forget to check out the lava ceilings, where turkeyfish and crustaceans are often found hiding upside down in the crevices. Outside the tubes you may find yellowmargin and whitemouth moray eels, friendly sea turtles and even rare critters such as leaf fish or giant anglerfish.

Christmas tree worms are light sensitive

59 BRENNECKE'S LEDGES

Location: *Makahuena point*
Depth Range: *60-90ft (18-27m)*
Access: *Boat*
Expertise Rating: *Intermediate*

Brennecke's Ledges (also known as Brennecke's Drop-Off) is located on Kauai's southeast shore, off Makahuena Point just east of Poipu. A large lava shelf runs parallel to the shore for several miles, its prime feature is a wall that drops down to 90ft. The top of the black lava shelf is beautifully studded with white and pink cauliflower coral. This area is always worth checking out for large Triton's trumpet shells, pincushion sea stars and small hermit crabs that often seek shelter within the protective branches of the coral.

As you drop down the wall, you'll find several black-coral trees and possibly endemic banded angelfish. Be sure to examine the numerous overhangs with your flashlight – you'll find many of the ceilings are entirely covered with brightly colored orange cup coral. Several types of nudibranchs feed on the cup coral and can often be found among the individual polyps. You may see another resident, the stunning orange-banded cowry.

Be sure to look for lobsters, reef crabs, squirrelfish and even whitetip reef sharks dozing underneath the overhangs. Schooling bluestripe snapper and green sea turtles can also be encountered at this site.

60   OCEANARIUM

Location: *Hanalei Bay*
Depth Range: *60-130ft (18-39m)*
Access: *Boat*
Expertise Rating: *Advanced*

Remote Oceanarium is one of Kauai's most exciting dives for advanced divers. Due to its locatation on the North Shore near the Na Pali Coast, the site is accessible only during summer by fast boat when the seas are calm, and is not offered by many charter operations.

Here you'll find three huge pinnacles that start at about 65ft and drop down to 120ft in front of a lava shelf. Large, dense schools of bluestripe snapper and other fish hover in the channels between the shelf and the pinnacles.

On the seaward side of the largest pinnacle, a sheer wall plummets beyond 130ft. This is perhaps the most dramatic area, where you'll find some beautiful black-coral trees. Use a flashlight to capture the colors of the black coral and the treasures they hide. Longnose hawkfish, with their stunning red-and-white-checker patterns, are often found within the branches.

The overhangs along the wall are encrusted with flower-like orange tube coral and may contain crabs such as giant hairy hermit crabs, nudibranchs and cowry shells. In the smaller *pukas* (crevices) along the wall look for the rare, endemic long-handed lobsters that favor this environment. This is also a great area to spot rare fish species such as morwongs and whiskered boarfish.

There's much to explore here but this is a deep dive, so be sure to check your time. Don't just rely on your dive guide to monitor your gauges: you are ultimately responsible for yourself. There is still plenty to see in the shallower areas, and if you look out into the blue you'll probably spot some uluas, barracuda or even manta and eagle rays.

Cauliflower coral with a diver in the background

61 TUNNELS REEF

Location: *Hanalei Bay*
Depth Range: *20-65ft (6-20m)*
Access: *Shore*
Expertise Rating: *Novice*

Unfortunately, due to high surf conditions, this popular shore diving and snorkeling spot is only accessible during summer. You'll find the best area to enter the water at the end of a dirt road off Highway 56, where a sign reading 'Right of way to beach' marks the turn-off.

New or less experienced divers should keep to the right, where there's a large sandy area surrounded by a coral reef. The bottom slopes down to only about 25ft, making it an ideal spot for novices to explore the reef overhangs and lava caverns and tunnels.

Experienced divers can swim to the left where the seafloor bottoms out at about 65ft. As you follow the contour of

Diver explores the ledges and overhangs found throughout Kauai's underwater world

the bottom, you'll come across several ledges, caves and overhangs along with a good range of fish life.

With luck you may encounter one of the resident whitetip reef sharks or sea turtles. In the sandy and rubble-covered patches you may find the unusual flying gurnard fish, razor wrasses and dragon wrasses. You are likely to experience a strong current here, which intensifies with depth.

62 KEE LAGOON

Location: *West of Hanalei Bay*
Depth Range: *10-30ft (3-9m)*
Access: *Shore*
Expertise Rating: *Novice*

Located on Kauai's North Shore just west of Haena Beach Park, this site can only be dived in summer when conditions are calm. Though there is no longer any coral here, you will find the shallow central area inside the lagoon a perfect snorkeling spot with lots of friendly fish and many juveniles seeking the shelter of the bay.

This is not a great scuba diving location due to the shallowness of the site, If you do decide to scuba dive, the best bet is to dive along either the left or the right side of the lagoon where the water is a little deeper. Novice divers should keep to the right, where currents are mostly absent.

In either direction you are likely to see schooling convict tangs (called *manini* in Hawaiian), butterflyfish and triggerfish, but to the left you'll find more ledges and a good variety of creatures.

On extremely calm days, experienced divers can swim through the lagoon and descend along the outside of the fringing reef. The water tends to be clear out here and is filled with caves, overhangs and a great abundance of fish.

Cleaning Stations

Observant divers will find a variety of symbiotic relationships throughout the marine world – associations in which two dissimilar organisms participate in a mutually beneficial relationship.

One of the most interesting relationships is found at cleaning stations, where one animal (or symbiont) advertises its grooming services to potential clients with inviting, undulating movements. Often this is done near a coral head or coral bommie.

Various species of cleaners such as wrasses and shrimp are dedicated to caring for their customers, which may include fish of all sizes and species. Larger fish, such as sharks and mantas, generally frequent cleaning stations serviced by angelfish, butterflyfish and larger wrasses, while turtles generally utilize the services of algae-feeding tangs that are eager to rid them of their algae build-up.

Customers hover in line until their turn comes. When the cleaner attends to a waiting customer – perhaps a grouper, parrotfish or even moray eel – it may enter the customer's mouth to perform dental hygiene, and even exit through the fish's gills. Although the customer could have an easy snack, it would never attempt to swallow the essential cleaner. The large fish benefit from the removal of parasites and dead tissue, while the little wrasses are provided with a meal.

By carefully approaching a cleaning station, divers will be able to get closer than is normally possible to many fish and observe behavior seen nowhere else on the reef.

Diver descends onto a large school of bluestripe snappers

63 | MANA CRACK

Location: *Southwest of Nahili Point*
Depth Range: *50-95ft (15-29m)*
Access: *Boat*
Expertise Rating: *Advanced*

Mana Crack is an exciting but weather-dependent dive, only likely to be accessible during summer. Located near the dramatic Na Pali Coast, it offers unusual terrain consisting of a reversed ledge deeper near shore and shallower on the seaward side.

Expect to see some gorgeous coral formations, including plate and antler corals, along with rare black-coral trees. Use your flashlight to explore the countless overhangs and small *pukas* (crevices) for lobsters, hermit crabs and cowry shells. You may even encounter some of the resident 'big boys' such as eagle rays, blacktip reef sharks and possibly even hammerhead sharks.

Tritons trumpets are a natural predator of the crown of thorns starfish

NIIHAU

The island of Niihau, located 17 miles (27km) southwest of Kauai, is the smallest of the main inhabited Hawaiian Islands. It earned the nickname the 'Forbidden Island' when it was closed to all but native Hawaiians in 1864 (when the island was privately purchased). Restrictions have become more lax and visitors are now allowed to take helicopter tours of the island.

A limited number of dive boats are also able to access the island's waters. A one- to 1¹/₂-hour channel crossing is necessary to reach Niihau and the nearby Lehua Rock, a slightly larger and more exciting version of Maui's Molokini Crater. Both Niihau and Lehua Rock boast breathtaking drop-offs, gigantic sea arches, canyons and caverns, most are best suited to advanced divers.

Niihau Dive Sites

	GOOD SNORKELING	NOVICE	INTERMEDIATE	ADVANCED
64 NIIHAU ARCHES				•
65 PYRAMID POINT			•	
66 VERTICAL AWARENESS				•
67 KEYHOLE				•

Diver with schooling eagle rays

64 NIIHAU ARCHES

Location: *East of Kikepa Point*
Depth Range: *20-80ft (6-24m)*
Access: *Boat*
Expertise Rating: *Advanced*

Perhaps Niihau's most popular and thrilling site, Niihau Arches gets its name from a principal feature – an immense archway at 35ft amid an underwater city of ridges, valleys and lava tubes. The largest tube extends into a huge chamber of around 100 sq ft. Longnose hawkfish inhabit the black feather coral and regular black coral found interspersed throughout the lava formations.

The site quickly drops as you swim out, providing an excellent area to watch large fish swim by: eagle rays, pelagic sharks (such as the occasional Galápagos shark), blacktip sharks and wahoos are among the site's visitors.

If you are familiar with local fish species, you will notice that this pristine site also boasts an abundance of otherwise rare fish, such as morwongs, and is also an excellent place to observe octopuses.

With some luck, you may even be able to observe a playful Hawaiian monk seal. These endemic mammals are highly endangered and should not be touched or harassed in any way.

Niihau has many archways and lava tubes to explore

65 PYRAMID POINT

Location: *Lehua rock*
Depth Range: *18-130ft (5-39m)*
Access: *Boat*
Expertise Rating: *Intermediate*

Pyramid Point – which lies opposite **Vertical Awareness** at Lehua Rock – is a fantastic wall that drops vertically from 18ft to about 180ft (below the recreational dive limit). On this generally easy drift dive, you can often see mantas, sharks, eagle rays and even Hawaiian monk seals. Although monk seals are curious and have been known to approach divers, be sure to keep a respectful distance and never chase or attempt to touch these rare, endangered mammals.

After you have used up your bottom time along the wall, slowly work your way back up to the top of the wall. From there, cruise through the channel between the wall and Lehua Rock on the steady tidal current. When timed right, this is a great thrill, with pyramid butterflyfish, pennant and lemon butterflyfish swirling all around you.

66 VERTICAL AWARENESS

Location: *Lehua Rock*
Depth Range: *40-130ft (12-39m)*
Access: *Boat*
Expertise Rating: *Advanced*

This site is one of the most thrilling and awe-inspiring sites in Hawaii. Advanced dive skills are a must when exploring this sheer-sided seamount that rises vertically from 280ft until it levels out at 40ft. The best features are found between 50ft and 100ft. Be sure to maintain neutral buoyancy throughout the dive and be aware of your depth at all times. The water is generally gin-clear, making depth perception very deceiving.

Along the wall you are likely to encounter dense schools of pennant butterflyfish, pyramid butterflyfish and tangs. The brilliantly hued endemic Hawaiian anthias and longfin anthias are regularly seen here.

Wreck of the Luckenbach

The *Andrea F. Luckenbach* was a 400ft freighter that hit a reef and sank off Kauai's east coast on March 4, 1951. Time and weather have taken their toll on the wreck, and the chains, 10ft anchors, propeller and boiler-room pieces are now scattered across the ocean floor. Squirrelfish and bigeyes seek shelter in the wreckage, while snapper and goatfish swim in midwater nearby.

Though the wreck can be dived from shore, the distance and unpredictable conditions make reaching it a challenge and visibility is limited. The *Luckenbach* should only be dived with a professional guide. Local dive operators may offer shore dives to the wreck from December to February.

In addition to small reef gems, this site is also well known for its big fish: graceful mantas, Galápagos sharks, huge uluas, wahoos, tunas and even Hawaiian monk seals all thrive in this environment. Be sure to periodically glance into the blue so you don't miss these large pelagic animals.

67 KEYHOLE

Location: *Lehua Rock*
Depth Range: *40-130ft (12-39m)*
Access: *Boat*
Expertise Rating: *Advanced*

This site gets it's name from the large split in the crater wall that resembles a keyhole from a distance. Experienced divers consider this one of the top dives in the Hawaiian islands due to the large fish action and the rare fish found here. Adorned with orange cup coral, the wall is known to host rare deep-water species, such as the endemic yellow anthias, normally found below 200ft. At this site, the beautiful fish frequents the area around a large black-coral bush together with the rare tinker butterfly fish. Gray reef sharks are often seen in packs of six or more. Take caution, as good surface skills are required due to strong currents and rough surface conditions. This dive is usually performed as a drift dive, which allows you to follow the current. Be sure to stay with your guide.

The endangered monk seal can often be seen at Niihau dive sites

It is common to find schooling pyramid butterflyfish associated with black coral

Marine Life

Diver approached by curious reef fish

The warm waters surrounding the Hawaiian islands are home to an incredible number of fish, coral and mammal species. Due to the archipelago's isolation, approximately 25% of the reef fish and many invertebrates are endemic (found nowhere else in the world). These unique creatures, along with Hawaii's fascinating underwater lava tubes and beautiful hard-coral gardens, are part of what makes diving in Hawaii special.

The animals pictured here are just a sample of the common vertebrates and invertebrates you are likely to find throughout the Hawaiin islands. Endemic species are listed separately.

Common names are used freely in the Hawaiian islands but are notoriously inaccurate and inconsistent. The two-part scientific name is much more accurate. This system is known as binomial nomenclature – the method of using two words (shown in italics) to identify an organism. The first word is the genus, into which members of similar species are grouped. The second word, the species, is the finest detail name and generally includes only organisms that can produce fertile offspring. Where the species or genus is unknown, the naming goes to the next known (and less specific) level: Family (F), Order (O), Class (Cl) or Phylum (Ph).

HAZARDOUS MARINE LIFE

Marine animals almost never attack divers, but many have defensive and offensive weaponry that can be triggered if they feel threatened or annoyed. The ability to recognize hazardous creatures is a valuable asset in avoiding accident and injury.

The following are some of the potentially hazardous creatures most commonly found in Hawaii.

Hydroid

Though hydroids come in many forms, in Hawaii you'll find only feather and fern hydroids, which grow on reefs and in crevices. They resemble tiny plants or feathers and generally look quite fragile and harmless; however, they can 'sting' by discharging small, specialized cells called nematocysts. Contact causes a burning sensation that lasts for several minutes and may produce red welts on the skin. Do not rub the area, as you will only spread the stinging particles. Cortisone cream can reduce the inflammation and antihistamine cream is good for killing the pain. Serious stings should be treated by a doctor.

Cone Shell

Do not touch or pick up cone shells. These mollusks, which are cone-like in shape with varying shell thickness and colour patterns, deliver a venomous sting by shooting a tiny poison dart from funnel-like proboscis. Stings will cause numbness and can be followed by muscular paralysis or even respiratory paralysis and heart failure. Immobilize the victim, apply a pressure bandage, be prepared to use CPR, and seek urgent medical aid.

Scorpionfish

There are no deadly stonefish in Hawaii but there are several types of scorpionfish. These well-camouflaged creatures have poisonous spines along their dorsal fins. They are often difficult to spot since they typically rest quietly on the bottom or on coral, looking like rocks. Practice good buoyancy control and watch where you put your hands. Wounds can be excruciating. To treat, wash the wound and immerse in non-scalding hot water for 30 to 90 minutes. Administer pain medications if necessary.

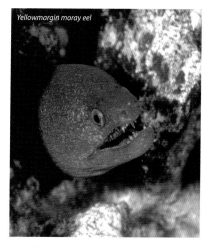
Yellowmargin moray eel

Lionfish

Also known as turkeyfish or firefish, these slow, graceful fish extend their feathery pectoral fins as they swim. They have distinctive vertical brown or black bands alternating with narrower pink or white bands. When threatened or provoked, lionfish may inject venom through dorsal spines that can penetrate booties, wetsuits and leather gloves. The wounds can be extremely painful. If stung, wash the wound and immerse in non-scalding hot water for 30 to 90 minutes. Administer pain medications if necessary.

Moray Eel

Moray eels are common on Hawaiian reefs. Distinguished by their long, thick, snake-like bodies and tapered heads, moray eels come in a variety of colors and patterns. Don't feed them or put your hand in a dark hole – eels have the unfortunate combination of sharp teeth and poor eyesight and will bite if they feel threatened. If you are bitten, don't try to pull your hand away suddenly – the teeth slant backward and are extraordinarily sharp. Let the eel release it and then surface slowly. Treat with antiseptics, anti-tetanus and antibiotics.

Crown of thorns are venomous and should not be han

Sea Urchin

Sea urchins tend to live in shallow areas near shore and come out of their shelters at night. They vary in coloration and size, with spines ranging from short and blunt to long and needle-sharp. The spines are the urchin's most dangerous weapon, easily able to penetrate neoprene wetsuits, booties and gloves.

There are a great variety of sea urchins in Hawaii. Many, but not all, have sharp spines. Divers should be most wary of the venomous spiny urchin, locally known as *wana*. They are generally black or black and white and have very long, brittle spines that break off easily. Puncture wounds immediately cause a throbbing pain. Treat minor punctures by extracting the spines and immersing the wound in non-scalding hot water. More serious injuries require medical attention.

Crown-of-Thorns

This large sea star may have up to 23 arms, although 13 to 18 are more commonly observed. Body coloration can be blue, green or grayish with the spines tinted red or orange. The spines

Stinging hydroids should be avoided

are venomous and can deliver a painful sting even if the animal has been dead for two or three days. Also beware the toxic pedicellariae (pincers) between the spines, which can also cause severe pain upon contact. To treat stings, remove any loose spines, soak the stung area in non-scalding hot water for 30 to 90 minutes and seek medical aid. Neglected wounds may produce serious injury. If you've been stung before, your reaction to another sting may be worse than the first.

Jellyfish

The waters of Hawaii contain no strongly toxic jellyfish. Jellyfish sting by releasing the stinging cells contained in their trailing tentacles. As a rule, the longer the tentacles, the more painful the sting. Stings are often irritating and not painful, but should be treated immediately with a decontaminant such as vinegar, rubbing alcohol, baking soda, meat tenderizer or diluted household ammonia. Be aware that some people may have a stronger reaction than others, in which case you should prepare to resuscitate and seek medical aid.

Portuguese Man-o-War

This colonial organism, distantly related to the jellyfish, is found at the surface, and is recognizable by its purplish, translucent 'floats' and long, trailing tentacles. Its tentacles, which can reach 50ft (15m) or more in length, are armed with exceedingly toxic stinging cells, which can cause a painful sting. Beached man-o-wars are still hazardous, even weeks after they've dried out and appear dead. Sting symptoms range from a mild itch to intense pain, blistering, skin discoloration, shock, breathing difficulties and even unconsciousness. If stung, apply a decontaminant such as vinegar, meat tenderizer or diluted household ammonia and seek immediate medical aid. Allergic reactions can be severe and life-threatening.

Travel Facts

Spinner dolphins are commonly seen from day boat charters throughout Hawaii

CLIMATE

Hawaii's climate is considered one of the most pleasant in the world. It is comfortably balmy and warm year-round, with northeasterly trade winds prevailing most of the year.

Average winter and summer temperatures vary by only 7°F (4°C). Near the coast, temperatures are between 68° and 83°F (20° and 28°C), though highland temperatures can be much cooler. Water temperatures range from a low of 72°F (22°C) in January to a high of 82°F (27°C) in August.

Generally, high mountains throughout the island chain block the trade winds and moisture-laden clouds that blow in from the northeast. These winds bring abundant rainfall to the windward side of the islands, while the leeward areas tend to receive only 10in to 25in (25cm to 64cm) of rain a year. The rainiest time of year for most of the islands is December to March, except along the Kona Coast on the Big Island, which experiences its wettest season during July and August.

LANGUAGE

English is the official language of Hawaii, though it is peppered with a mixture of colorful Hawaiian phrases and words borrowed from the various immigrant languages. It is also common to hear islanders use pidgin (a modern and ever-changing local slang based on a simplified form of English) to communicate with each other.

The only place where Hawaiian is still the primary language is on the privately owned island of Niihau, but many Hawaiian names, words and expressions are still commonly used throughout the islands. In fact, some 85% of all place names in Hawaii are in Hawaiian and often have interesting translations and stories behind them. Though Hawaiian words may seem long and complicated, the written language has just 12 letters. Pronunciation and meaning are indicated through glottal stops (') and macrons (short, straight lines over some vowels), though these are often omitted in modern texts.

GETTING THERE

Hawaii is a major transportation hub for the Pacific, connecting distant shores on all sides. Nearly all flights to Hawaii enter via the Honolulu International Airport on Oahu, which is serviced daily by major carriers from the US mainland, Asia, Australia, Canada, New Zealand and the South Pacific. Some of the outer islands also have direct flights to the US mainland and Asia, but the schedules are less reliable and change with demand.

GATEWAY CITY – HONOLULU

Honolulu (population approximately 400,000), is the state's capital and center of business, culture and politics. Honolulu's ethnic diversity can be seen on every corner.

Its eclectic mix of sleek high-rises and Victorian-era buildings combine well with the Spanish-style City Hall, the missionary churches and the Royal Palace. Many interesting and historic sites are within walking distance of each other. Though the greater Honolulu area has seen tremendous growth during the 20th century, the downtown area near the harbor remains the heart of the city.

Since the late 1700s, Honolulu has provided a safe harbor for international travelers, many of whom have made this their home. Honolulu International Airport and Honolulu Harbor are Hawaii's busiest ports.

Just south of downtown Honolulu is Waikiki, a 1.5 mile-long stretch of golden beach lined with countless hotels, restaurants, bars and shops. As Hawaii's first tourist destination, Waikiki still accommodates nearly half of the state's visitors.

Honolulu is the gateway city to the Hawaiian Islands

Keauhou Bay, Big Island

GETTING AROUND

The usual method for traveling from one island to another is by plane. Aloha, Hawaiian Airlines and Island Air are the major inter-island carriers that service the five major airports – Honolulu (on Oahu), Kona and Hilo (on the Big Island), Kahului (on Maui) and Lihue (on Kauai). Hawaiian Airlines and Island Air also fly to Molokai and Lanai (in Maui County), while Island Air services the smaller airport on Maui at Kapalua.

Hawaii Superferry (www.hawaiisuperferry.com) is scheduled to begin a daily service to Oahu, Maui and Kauai in 2007, while daily service to the Island of Hawaii is scheduled to begin in 2009. These Superferries will be over 300ft long and carry over 800 passengers and up to 280 vehicles. If this venture goes well, it will likely change the travel habits of locals with families on other islands. Refer to the website for updated information. To get around each of the islands, it's best to travel by rental car. Taxis can be quite costly and public transportation is limited, except on Oahu, where you will find an extensive bus system and the meaning of 'Hawaiian Time.'

ENTRY

The conditions for entering Hawaii are the same as for entering any other state in the United States. US citizens should carry valid photo ID. Citizens of countries that are participants in the Visa Waiver Program (VWP) may enter the US for up to 90 days with a valid passport without obtaining a visa first. (For more information about the VWP, refer to the visa section at http://travel.state.gov. Visitors from all other countries must have a valid passport from their home country and a valid US visa (obtainable through a US consulate or embassy).

MONEY

The US dollar ($US) is the only accepted currency. All major credit cards and traveler's checks in US$ are widely accepted throughout Hawaii.

Tipping in Hawaii is the same as in the rest of the US. The standard rate for restaurant service and taxi drivers is 10% to 20%, and hotel bellhops should be given at least $1 per bag.

TIME

Hawaii is just east of the international date line. When it's noon in Hawaii, it is 2pm in San Francisco, 10pm in London and 8am the next day in Sydney. Hawaii does not observe daylight saving time, so the time difference is one hour greater during those months when other countries observe daylight saving. Being on 'Hawaiian Time' means living at a very laid-back pace, though it's sometimes used as an excuse for being late.

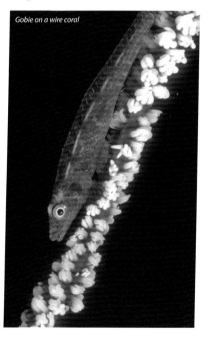
Gobie on a wire coral

Riding Oahu's big waves

ELECTRICITY

Electricity is the same as on the US mainland: 110 volts, 60 cycles. Two-pronged flat plugs (some with a third, round grounding prong) are used. Some electronics and department stores sell voltage converters and plug adapters, but it is best to bring your own.

Remember that many electronic chargers can be switched, or switch automatically, from 110 volts to 220 volts and vice versa.

WEIGHTS & MEASURES

The imperial system of measurement is used throughout Hawaii. Distances are in inches, feet, yards and miles. Weights are in ounces, pounds and tons. Air pressure on scuba gauges is read in pounds per square inch (PSI) and underwater depth is read in feet. See the conversion chart on the inside of the back cover of this guide for metric equivalents.

Both imperial and metric measurements are given in this guide, except for specific references within the dive site descriptions, which are represented in imperial units only.

BUSINESS HOURS

On all of the major islands you'll find convenience stores and grocery stores that are open 24 hours a day. Drugstores usually open at 9am and close late in the evening.

Tourist-oriented stores often open at 10am and close at 10pm. Though most

A special weather condition that can occur on all islands is called 'kona weather' or 'kona winds.' (Kona means leeward in Hawaiian.) During kona weather, the winds shift from the typical northeast trade wind direction and blow instead from the south. Kona weather is fairly rare, occurring only a few days a year during the winter months. What makes it special and significant to divers is that it opens up dive sites inaccessible under normal (trade wind) conditions. The ocean swell patterns change at this time – snorkeling spots suddenly become surfing spots and vice versa.

Islanders greet each other with the shaka sign, which is made by folding down the three middle fingers to the palm and extending the thumb and little finger. The hand is then usually held up and shaken in greeting. It's as common as waving.

banks are open from 8:30am to 4:30pm, many offer extended service one or two days a week, and some are even open on Saturday. Automated teller machines (ATMs) can be found outside banks and in grocery stores throughout the islands.

Aloha Airlines; ☎ 808-484-1111
Hawaiian Airlines; ☎ 808-838-1555
Island Air; ☎ 808-484-2222

ACCOMMODATION

Hawaii offers everything from the most elegant and luxurious resorts to simple hotels with shared bathrooms. Many dive operators offer packages in conjunction with mid- to high-priced hotels or condominiums. Major resorts usually have their own integrated dive operation.

Romantics can opt to stay in bed and breakfasts (B&Bs), which vary in price and can be found on most islands, some even cater to divers and snorkelers.

There are numerous public campgrounds on the islands, but few privately-owned campgrounds are available. Theft and violent crime are not common, though campers – especially those traveling alone – should be cautious.

Campgrounds that are well established, have caretakers and attract other campers are always good bets.

DINING & FOOD

Hawaii offers an array of dining options, from international gourmet cuisine to American fast food. Continental or European restaurants are found in most hotels and Asian restaurants are common. Most restaurants offer at least a few fresh seafood dishes. The *luau* is a buffet-style meal that features *kalua*, a whole pig cooked in an *imu* (an oven dug into the ground). Tourists can participate in a commercial version of this celebration, which is offered as a dinner show at large hotels and resorts.

The 'plate lunch' is popular with the locals and consists of two scoops of rice, a scoop of macaroni salad and a generous portion of teriyaki chicken, *kalua* pig, Spam or other meat dish. Fish, pork and taro wrapped in a *ti* leaf is known as *laulau*. Taro is also used to make *poi*, a paste pounded from cooked taro and water. *Pupus* is the word used for appetizers, such as *poke* (marinated raw fish), *limu* (seaweed) salad, sashimi or anything else used as hors d'oeuvres.

SHOPPING

With Hawaii's endless souvenir options you'll be able to shop to your heart's content. You'll find everything from T-shirts and plastic hula dancers to dolphin statues and beautiful wooden bowls hand-crafted from native wood.

Black-coral jewelry and shell ornaments are found in most tourist shops. It is illegal in Hawaii to remove stony coral from the reefs, but black coral is fair game throughout the state.

Before purchasing black-coral products, understand that live black coral is harvested to create jewelry, resulting in the depletion of this stunning coral. The same considerations must be contemplated when purchasing shell products. Most shell products are not made from shells that were washed up on the beach, but rather from live animals taken from the reefs. Buying such products only encourages the depletion of the oceans' natural resources and lessens the beauty and biodiversity of the reefs.

Child plays on traditional Hawaiian outrigger canoe

Hanauma Bay, Oahu

Listings

DIVING SERVICES

There are countless diving services available throughout the Hawaiian Islands. It is common for new services to start up, dive shops to change owners or merge, and of course close. The following is a broad (but not exhaustive) list of services available in each of the regions covered in this guide. Though mailing addresses are provided for contact purposes, most operators now have a presence on the internet and do many of their bookings online or by phone. Please note that it is always wise to contact the dive shops directly for exact locations and specific services.

Most dive services offer a range of rental and retail gear, airfills and guided shore and/or boat dives. Many offer certification and advanced diving classes and will accept Open Water referrals, and all facilities should display their appropriate affiliations (NAUI, PADI, SSI etc.). Most major credit cards are accepted.

OAHU

Aaron's Dive Shops
307 Hahani Street, Kailua, HI 96734
☎ 1888-84-SCUBA ☎ 262-2333
www.hawaii-scuba.com

Aloha Dive Shop
377 Keahole St. #E-101
Hawaii Kai, HI 96825
www.alohadiveshop.com

AquaZone SCUBA diving & Water Sports Center
Outrigger Waikiki on the
Beach Hotel & Waikiki Beach
Marriott Resort
☎ 866-923-3484
www.aquazone.net

Breeze Hawaii Diving Adventures
3014 Kaimuki Ave
Honolulu, HI 96816
☎ 735-1857, ☎ 735-1360
www.breezehawaii.com/english/

Captain Bruce's Scuba Charters
994 Waihole St.
Honolulu, HI 96821
☎ 373-3590, ☎ 800-535-2487
www.captainbruce.com

Island Divers Hawaii
PO Box 30108
Honolulu HI 96820
☎ 888-844-3483, ☎ 808-423-8222
www.oahuscubadiving.com

Ocean Concepts
☎ 800-808-3483
www.oceanconcepts.com

Oahu Dive Center
345 Hahani St
Kailua, Hi 96734
☎ 1-866-933-DIVE
www.oahudivecenter.com

Reef Trekkers Hawaii
Scuba Diving Tours
Honolulu HI
☎ 96830-8899 USA, ☎ 877-FLY-REEF
Outside US ☎ 943-0588
www.reeftrekkers.com

See in Sea Scuba
670 Auahi Street, Suite A-1
Honolulu, Hawaii 96813-5166
☎ 1-866-528-2311, ☎ 808-528-2311
www.divehawaii.com

Waikiki Dive Center
424 Nahua Street
Honolulu, Hawaii 96815
☎ 808-922-2121
www.WaikikiDiving.com

BIG ISLAND

Aloha Dive Company
PO Box 4454
Kailua-Kona, HI 96740
☎ 325-5560, ☎ 800-708-KONA
www.alohadive.com

A Sea Paradise
RO Box 580
Kailua-Kona, HI 96740
☎ 322-2500, ☎ 800-322-5662
www.seaparadise.com

Big Island Divers
75-5467 Kaiwi St
Kailua-Kona, HI 96740
☎ 329-6068, ☎ 800-488-6068
www.bigislanddivers.com

Body Glove Cruisers
PO Box 4523
Kailua-Kona, HI 96740
☎ 326-7122, ☎ 800-551-8911
www.bodyglovehawaii.com

Breeze Hawaii Diving (Kona)
74-5543 Kaiwi St, Suite 115
Kailua-Kona, HI 96740
☎ 326-4085
www.breezehawaii.com/english/

Dive Makai Charters
PO Box 2955
Kailua-Kona, HI 96745
☎ 808-329-2025
www.divemakai.com

Fair Wind
78-7130 Kaleiopapa St.
Kailua-Kona, HI 96740
☎ 322-2788
www.fair-wind.com

Kona Honu Divers Inc
PO Box 390190
Kailua-Kona, HI 96739
☎ 1-888-333-4668 or ☎ 808-324-4668
www.konahonudivers.com

Hualalai Watersports
PO Box 383657
Waikoloa, HI 96738
☎ 325-8221
www.divesail.com

Jack's Diving Locker
75-5813 Alii Drive
Kailua-Kona, Hawaii 96740
☎ 808-329-7585 or ☎ 800-345-4807
dive@jacksdivinglocker.com

Kohala Divers Ltd.
Kawaihae Shopping Center
PO Box 44940
Kawaihae, HI 96743
☎ 808-882-7774
www.kohaladivers.com

Mauna Lani Sea Adventures, Inc.
68-1400 Maunalani Dr.
Kohala Coast, HI 96743
☎ 885-7883
www.hawaiiseaadventures.com

Nautilus Dive Center, Inc.
382 Kamehameha Ave. #102
Hilo, HI 96720
☎ 935-6939
www.nautilusdivehilo.com

Ocean Sports Waikoloa
69-275 Waikoloa Beach Dr.
Kohala Coast, HI 96738
☎ 808-886-6666, ☎ 888-724-5234
www.hawaiioceansports.com

Planet Ocean Watersports
200 Kanoelehua Aye, Unit 8
Hilo, HI 96720
☎ 935-7277 www.islandsource.com/
diving/divesnork1.htm

Red Sails Sports Hawaii
425 Waikoloa Beach Drive
Waikoloa, Hawaii 96738
☎ 808-886-2876
www.redsailhawaii.com

Sandwich Isle Divers
75-5729 Alii Dr, Suite 1
Kailua-Kona, HI 96740
☎ 808-329-9188
☎ 888-743-3483
www.sandwichisledivers.com

MAUI

5 Star Scuba
Corporate Office
www.fivestarscuba.com

Bill's Scuba Shack
2349 S. Kihei Rd. Kihei, HI 96753
☎ 808-891-0500, ☎ 877-213-4488
www.scubashack.com

Dive Maui
900 Front St.
Lahaina, HI 96761
☎ 808-667-2080, ☎ 866-821-7450
www.divemaui.com

Ed Robinson's Diving Adventures
PO. Box 616 Kihei, HI 96753
☎ 879-3584
☎ 800-635-1273
www.mauiscuba.com

Extended Horizons
94 Kupuohi #A-1
Lahaina Hawaii 96761
☎ 667-0611
☎ 888-DIVE MAUI
www.scubadivemaui.com

Island Explorations
(Snorkeling Tours)
RO. Box 1107
Makawao, HI 96768
☎ 808-572-8437
www.maui.net/~annf/index.html

Lahaina Divers, Inc.
143 Dickenson St
Lahaina, HI 96761
☎ 667-7496
☎ 800-998-3483
www.lahainadivers.com

Maui Dive Shops
1455 S. Kihei Rd.
Kihei, HI 96753
☎ 808-879-1775
☎ (800) 542-3483
www.mauidiveshop.com

Maui Diving Scuba Center
222 Papalaua St, Suite 112
Lahaina, HI 96761
☎ 667-0633
☎ (800) 959-7319
www.mauidiving.com

Maui Sun Divers
PO Box 565
Kihei, HI 96753
☎ 808-879-3337
☎ 877-879-3337
www.mauisundivers.com

Mike Severns Diving
PO Box 627
Kihei, HI 96753
☎ 879-6596
www.mikesevernsdiving.com

Pacific Dive Maui
150 Dickenson St
Lahaina, HI 96761
☎ 667-5331
☎ 877-667-7331
www.pacificdive.com

Tropical Divers Maui
RO. Box 11415
Lahaina, HI 96761
☎ (808) 669-6284
☎ (800) 994-6284
www.scubamaui.com

KAUAI & NIIHAU

Blue Dolphin Charters Ltd
PO Box 869
Eleele, Kauai 96705
☎ 808-335-5553
☎ 877-511-1311
www.kauaiboats.com

Bubbles Below Scuba Charters
☎ 808-332-7333
☎ 866-kaimanu
www.bubblesbelowkauai.com

Dive Kauai Scuba Center
1038 Kuhio Highway
Kapaa, HI 96746
☎ 808-822-0452
☎ (800) 828-3483
www.divekauai.com

Fathom Five Divers
RO. Box 907, 3450 Poipu Rd.
Koloa, HI 96756
☎ 742-6991
☎ 800-972-3078
www.fathomfive.com

Mana divers
PO Box 500
Eleele, HI 96705
☎ 808-742-9849
☎ 877-348-3669
www.manadivers.com

Seasport Divers
PO Box 638
Koloa, HI 96756
☎ 800-685-5889,
☎ 808-742-9303
www.seasportdivers.com

Snorkel Bob's (Kauai)
Kapaa
4-734 Kuhio Hwy, Kapaa, HI 96746
☎ 808-823-9433
Koloa
3236 Poipu Rd, Koloa, HI
☎ 808-742-2206
www.snorkelbob.com

Sunrise Scuba
1038 Kuhio Hwy, Kapaa, HI 96746
☎ 822-7333,
☎ 800-695-DIVE
Fax: 823-6515
www.sunrisediving.com

LIVE-ABOARDS

Kona Aggressor II
Live/Dive Pacific, Inc.
74-5588 Pawai P1, Building F
Kailua-Kona, HI 96740
☎ 329-8182
☎ 800-344-5662
www.pac-aggressor.com
Home port: Kailua-Kona
Description: 80ft
Destinations: West coast of the Big Island
Season: All
Passengers: 10 (5 state rooms, queen and single bed in each, private shower and bath)
Other: 7-day trips ($5^{1}/_{2}$ dive days), 5 dives per day, onboard photo center and E-6 processing, handicapped accessible.

Sunseeker
PO Box 383657
Waikoloa, HI 96738
☎ 808-325-8221
www.divesail.com
Home port: Honokahau Harbor
Description: 61ft
Destinations: South Point to Waipio Valley on the Big Island
Season: All
Passengers: 4-6 (master suite and Vberth with private bathrooms)
Other: 1- to 7-day custom trips.

Index

THIS IS NOT
THE END

www.lonelyplanet.com

CHAT TO OTHER TRAVELLERS • GIVE US FEEDBACK • GET EXTRA
DESTINATION INFORMATION • BOOK FLIGHTS, ACCOMMODATION
AND EVERYTHING ELSE • PLAN TRIPS • BUY THINGS • AND MORE